LEARNING TO LEAD

A Primer on Economic Development Strategies

Maury Forman

and

James Mooney

*with contributions by Charles Eckenstahler
and Dionne Maniotes Hulsey*

illustrations by

David Horsey

WASHINGTON STATE
COMMUNITY, TRADE AND
ECONOMIC DEVELOPMENT

Building Foundations For The Future

*This project was funded with assistance from the
U.S.D.A. Forest Service, Rural Community Assistance Program*

KENDALL/HUNT PUBLISHING COMPANY
4050 Westmark Drive   Dubuque. Iowa 52002

CONTENTS

Acknowledgments iv

Author and Contributor Notes v

SECTION I — ORGANIZATIONAL DEVELOPMENT 1

    1   The Five Cornerstones 3
    2   Establishing an Economic
        Development Program 9

SECTION II — PRODUCT DEVELOPMENT 25

    3   Infrastructure 27
    4   Gateway Programs 39
    5   Downtown Revitalization 49
    6   Business Parks 59
    7   Speculative Buildings 69

SECTION III — MARKET DEVELOPMENT 75

    8   New Resident Attraction 77
    9   Partnerships 87

SECTION IV — BUSINESS DEVELOPMENT 95

    10   Business Retention and Expansion 97
    11   Business Attraction 109
    12   Start-ups and Emerging Enterprises 121
    13   Tourism 133

SECTION V — WORKFORCE DEVELOPMENT 143

    14   Workforce Development 145

SECTION VI — DECISION 159

    15   Decision Time 161

ACKNOWLEDGMENTS

Dennie Houle, the driving force behind the development of this book, has been a constant advocate for education and training materials. In working with community decision-makers, he has been instrumental in seeing that basic relevant information is included in their programs. His input into this manuscript was sometimes irritating but always essential. He encouraged and challenged us, which greatly improved the manuscript, and we sincerely appreciate his efforts.

Few economic developers are well-versed in *all* areas of the profession. We are therefore fortunate to have had a number of people help with the writing and made this publication possible. Chuck Eckenstahler, Dionne Hulsey, and Karen Ball wrote the first drafts of several chapters and gave direction to the manuscript. We appreciate their input, time, and understanding of the changes we made to their text. We also offer our appreciation and thanks to Udaya Patnaik, John Niles, Dick Larman, Dave Wingate, Susan Kempf, Rita Robison, and Sally Ledgerwood for assisting with the edits, rewrites, and reviews of the chapters. Their expertise in economic development and experience in working with boards helped make this a more practical book for decision-makers.

We owe a great deal of gratitude to Jennifer Williams, Russ Campbell, and Neal VanDeventer for their technical assistance, Suzanne Villmain for the cover design, Connie Dotan and Betsy Gilder for their encouragement, Marianne Williamson for her inspirational support, and Monica Hautzenrader and Evelyn Roehl for their excellent editorial support that made this book reader-friendly. Without these people, this book would never have come to fruition.

We are indebted to David Horsey, the 1999 Pulitzer Prize Winner in Editorial Cartooning, for the wonderful cartoons that complement each chapter. Working with David made this book fun—just as economic development should be for the readers of this publication.

Two publications were extremely useful in creating this book. The first, *Introduction to Economic Development*, is a manual developed by the Council for Urban Economic Development, for their basic course. This manual and the class for which it was prepared are excellent resources for economic development practitioners and boards. We encourage those who want to learn more about economic development to attend this excellent training course. The second publication, *Economic Development: A Strategic Approach for Local Governments*, by Don Morrison of the Local Government Institute in Tacoma, Washington, published by the International City/County Management Association, is an excellent manual for local governments that want to develop a strategic economic development plan. We thank Don and Jeffrey Finkle, President/CEO of the Council for Urban Economic Development, for allowing us to use some of their material in this book.

The U.S.D.A. Forest Service, Rural Community Assistance Program, whose staff is dedicated to working with communities in developing healthy economies, funded this project. The authors appreciate their financial support and the technical assistance they provide throughout the Northwest.

Finally, we offer our love and appreciation to our families, Gail, Jamie, Jordan, Shane, Mary, Josh, and Adam, who have endured lengthy phone calls, late nights at the office, and weekends at the computer. Their patience will be rewarded with our promise of not writing another book...until the next one.

Authors

Maury Forman, Ph.D

Maury Forman is the Program Manager for Education and Training for the Washington State Department of Community, Trade and Economic Development. He is also the Course Director for the nationally-accredited Northwest Economic Development Games.

He is the recipient of numerous awards, including the 1997 Richard Preston Award for outstanding contributions in educational advancement for economic development practitioners; the 1998 ROI Research Institute Award for Innovation in Adult Education; and the 1998 Vision 2000 Award from the U.S. Small Business Administration Office of Advocacy for excellent programming in education and training.

Dr. Forman is also the author/editor of several publications, including: *The Race To Recruit, The Washington Entrepreneurs Guide, The Washington State Business Resource Directory, How To Create Jobs Now and Beyond 2000, Keeping Business Happy Healthy and Local, Back to Basics Management,* and *Cartooning Washington: A Cartoon History of the Evergreen State.*

James Mooney, CED

Jim Mooney has been a practicing economic developer for 19 years in the private and public sector in Michigan and Indiana. He is currently president of Development Services, a full-service economic development consulting agency in northwest Indiana.

Mr. Mooney has a Masters Degree from Michigan State University. He has now published three books on economic development focused on business attraction, deal negotiation, and successful program implementation. He also instructs deal-negotiating classes at five universities throughout the United States, an experience that has honed his technical knowledge and presentation skills.

Prior to starting his own consulting practice, Mr. Mooney worked for NIPSCO Industries' economic development department. During this period he became the first and only Certified Economic Developer in northwest Indiana, a distinction he holds to this day.

Contributors

Charles Eckenstahler

Charles Eckenstahler has more than 25 years experience in municipal planning, economic development, and consulting to various municipalities in seven states. Mr. Eckenstahler served four years (1973-1977) as a County Planning Director and seven years (1977-1984) as a Regional Planning Director. In 1989, he founded Public Consulting Team, a municipal consulting service with offices in Michigan City, Indiana, and Benton Harbor, Michigan.

Mr. Eckenstahler is the author of more than 100 articles on various real estate and planning issues and has been a speaker at numerous state and national association meetings. He is often sought after for opinions on municipal planning and real estate matters for such publications as *ULI Development, National Real Estate Investor, Midwest Real Estate News, Crains Detroit Business, Detroit Free Press, Planning and Zoning News,* and *Lawyers Weekly.*

Dionne Maniotes Hulsey

Dionne Maniotes Hulsey has many years of sales and marketing experience in the tourism industry. She is currently the Group Sales Manager for Blue Chip Casino, Inc. Prior to joining the Blue Chip in July 1997, Ms. Hulsey served as Executive Director for the I-80/90 Tourism Development Commission, a regional tourism organization targeted toward increasing the economic impact of visitor-related spending in northern Indiana. Her responsibilities at the I-80/90 Commission included managing all aspects of the commission, developing a successful sales campaign, writing and administering grants, developing visitor information guides, and coordinating various traveler-related programs.

Ms. Hulsey has also served as Sales Manager of the Airport Hilton Hotel in Indianapolis, Indiana; Director of Sales and Marketing at the Holiday Inn in Lebanon, Indiana; and Director of Transportation and Tourism for Union Station Associates in Indianapolis, Indiana. She has a degree from Purdue University.

ABSTRACT

Learning to Lead: A Primer on Economic Development Strategies, provides a general overview of the major issues related to economic development. The intent of this book is to help decision-makers make informed choices regarding their community strategies.

To receive copies of this publication, please write:

**Washington Department of
Community, Trade and Economic Development
Education and Training Program
2001 Sixth Avenue, Suite 2600
Seattle, WA 98121**

SECTION I.

ORGANIZATIONAL DEVELOPMENT

Chapter 1: THE FIVE CORNERSTONES

Guiding Principles:

☞ Economic development is comprised of five cornerstones: organizational, product, market, business, and workforce.

☞ Successful communities that choose to expand their economies incorporate elements of all five cornerstones.

☞ Economic development is an investment in the future of your community.

☞ Communities should recognize and understand their individual assets.

☞ Economic development plans must have community consensus.

☞ Partnerships are an essential component of all five cornerstones.

☞ External partners will be able to assist a community in education and training, funding, technical and organizational assistance, and incentives.

After attending a conference for newly elected mayors in the state capitol, Rose had a lot to think about on her drive home. New laws would impact cities throughout the state, and other legislative issues, such as project funding or lack of it in certain regions, now seemed vitally important. In an hour, she would be back in Field, a city of just under 10,000 people.

During the conference, she noticed how many other representatives were from communities which the state had defined as "small" and "rural." She could have told them that. After all, she had grown up in Field and was proud to be the third generation running the family nursery business. Although she had left to go to college, where she met her husband Bob, she eventually moved back home. She and Bob had expanded the original retail business to include a wholesale division and a small mail-order catalog. It provided a good living for them, her parents, and her sister.

As she drove through other towns, she wondered about what made them unique. Some looked the same as they had 20 years ago, while others looked more prosperous, with new buildings here and there or new sidewalks down Main Street; one town even had a new manufacturing plant. She also reflected on all the things she learned at the conference. They had talked about economic development, what it meant, and the need for organizing community groups to do some planning.

She began to think about Field's future. Everyone knew the manufacturing plant—the largest employer in the area—was going to close; it was just a matter of time. Her brother had worked there since graduating from high school, as did her sister's husband. No one knew exactly what would happen after it shut down. The owners were making what they considered the best business decision for their interests, but that wasn't going to lessen the impact on Field, a conservative community with good schools, low crime rate, and historically slow, steady economic growth. Many of the kids left after they graduated, but others, like Rose, came back home to work and raise their families. Now, the talk at all the coffee shops was about the coming "doom and gloom."

Rose loved her town—that's why she had run for mayor. The previous mayor, who held the office for 20 years before retiring, made few changes because things seem to be going okay. She believed she could help Field weather the coming changes by providing a new perspective. She also knew it was not going to be easy. Many folks were set in their ways.

Her parents had balked when she and Bob wanted to make changes at the nursery, but eventually agreed to look at things with a long-term perspective in hopes that their grandchildren would also stay in Field and work in the family business. Rose felt that running a local government was no different than managing a business, and those same methods could work with the town.

But how could she get things moving in Field? She stopped for gas and a cup of coffee. Putting together an economic development planning group might work. It could be made up of "stakeholders" in the community—the entities, agencies, businesses, and interested parties that made up the local economy. Rose knew that it needed to be balanced and representative, but who would be key members who could bring their perspectives and unique knowledge? Who understood what economic development really meant and—most important—who would be willing to work together to get things done? Rose took the napkin from her coffee and started writing down the names of potential members of the group.

As she got back in her car, Rose felt excited. She knew it would take work, but she could picture companies growing, new businesses starting up, and lots of new jobs. She allowed herself to dream about Field's future as she headed up the road.

Welcome to Economic Development

Does the above scenario sound familiar? Does the town of Field seem a lot like where you live? Did you get a call by a friend or colleague asking you to serve on an economic development committee or board?

There are hundreds of rural communities just like Field and thousands of people just like you. Everywhere, people want to understand the issues affecting the local economy, improve the business climate, and provide jobs for the next generation.

Only three things can happen to your local economy:

> 1 *Economic expansion*
> 2 *Economic stagnation*
> 3 *Economic contraction*

If your community decides to expand, you will need to:

- ▶ *Explain to your community why economic development is important.*
- ▶ *Understand the obstacles, opportunities, and critical issues of your community.*
- ▶ *Identify existing programs, people, and resources.*
- ▶ *Articulate an agreed-upon vision for your community.*

This book identifies the most essential issues facing communities today and will help you focus on and decide which economic development strategies will work best. Learn the basics of each, then pick the programs most applicable to your community and its vision.

What is Economic Development?

Economic development is a program, a group of policies, or activity that seeks to improve the economic well-being and quality of life for a community. Ideally, it will create and retain jobs that facilitate growth and provide a stable tax base. Economic development programs can take numerous approaches. No single strategy, policy, or program can assure success for a community. Some communities will succeed, while others will have to develop their assets to become marketable.

In order to create an effective program that works for the local economy, the community must understand the five levels of development. Each level consists of various strategies that can be implemented based on their geography, economy, and politics.

Organizational Development	*Creating and maintaining a recognized and legitimate forum for exchanging ideas and addressing the needs of the community. This will allow you to set a strategy, raise funds, and work with partners in a more efficient manner.*
Product Development	*Investments that are maintained, upgraded, or developed by labor and capital to improve the community. This may include infrastructure, downtown areas, gateways, business parks, or speculative buildings.*
Market Development	*Activities that focus on recruiting individuals who would enhance the economy, such as retired citizens or lone eagles, and enlarging the market area in which they could receive products and services.*
Business Development	*Programs that nurture businesses growth and investment. These are often the core of most economic development activities and include business attraction, retention and expansion, tourism, and start-up and emerging businesses.*
Workforce Development	*Policies that build the skills of its local workforce. This includes partnerships between business, education, and government so that all residents can be contributing members of the local economy.*

Why is Economic Development Important?

Historically, the local economy was looked at as something that had a presence, but for which citizens had no opportunity to influence. Today, however, we believe that active citizens can directly shape the economy, and the community will benefit in numerous ways:

Increased Tax Base	Additional revenue to support, maintain, and improve local services such as roads, parks, libraries, and emergency medical services.
Job Development	To provide better wages, benefits, and opportunities for advancement.
Business Retention	Businesses that feel appreciated by the community and, in turn, feel as if they are contributing to the economy will stay in town.
Economic Diversification	Helps expand the economy and reduces a community's vulnerability to a single business sector.
Self-sufficiency	Public services would be less dependent on intergovernmental transfers that change with each election.
Productive Use of Property	Property used for its "highest and best use" maximizes the productivity of that property.
Quality of Life	More local tax dollars and jobs raise the economic tide for the community, which generally increases the overall standard of living of the residents.
Recognition of Local Products	Oftentimes, successful economic development will occur when locally produced goods are consumed to a greater degree in the local market.

Membership on local economic development boards or committees—indeed, their very existence—is testimony to the belief that people can and do make a difference when they actively participate in shaping local economies.

Understanding the Players

Starting a local economic development organization can feel like a daunting task. While it will be a significant undertaking for a community, remember that you're not going at it alone. The players are numerous and are located at all layers of government and society.

THE FIVE CORNERSTONES
OF ECONOMIC DEVELOPMENT:

Organizational · Product · Market · Business · Workforce

ARE SUPPORTED BY:

Federal Government:	State Government:	Local Government:
Department of Commerce: Economic Development Administration	Departments of: Commerce/ Economic Development	County Cities
Department of Agriculture: Forest Service Rural Development	Transportation Labor Agriculture	**Associations:** Main Street Program American Economic Development Council
Small Business Administration: Small Business Development Centers	Employment Security Ecology	Council for Urban Economic Development National Business Incubation Association
Department of Labor: Employment and Training	**Strategic Partners:**	**Special Authorities:**
	Utilities	Community Development Corporations
	Community Colleges	
Department of Interior: Bureau of Indian Affairs	Universities	Public Development Authorities
	Voc-Tech Schools	
	Economic Development Councils	Port Districts
	Private Industry Councils	
	Public-Private Partnerships	

Internal economic development partners—local individuals, agencies, businesses, and civic groups—are essential for creating a winning team. External economic development partners—organizations and agencies based outside of the community—also play an active role and can assist and support all five cornerstones. The key is to identify who they may be, then isolate their roles and develop a program which:

> ▶ Coordinates their contribution to the community, and
> ▶ Provides any missing services at the local level.

Usually this support comes in the form of:

Education and training
Organization assistance
Funding
Incentives
Technical assistance

Identifying and contacting these groups very early in the process will help ensure their support and cooperation for your economic development efforts. The more resources a community has, the greater potential there is for your community to succeed.

∞

What Success Looks Like

Mayor Rose contacted all the people whose names she had written on her napkin: several business owners, an educator, a go-getter civic booster, a former softball coach, a successful real estate agent, an outspoken environmental activist, and others. She selected this diverse group of individuals because she knew each would bring a unique perspective to the formation of an economic development program.

Every person she asked agreed to participate in the economic development planning group. They were enthusiastic about being involved in their community's future. Each planning committee member had her or his own vision of what they would like the town to be. They all had ideas about how to achieve their personal goals. But they also realized that to be successful as a community they would need to understand more about the five cornerstones.

Although they were eager to recruit a company to replace the closing plant, they also knew that Field had some serious shortcomings. They were disappointed to learn that no model economic development program existed. Every community was different, and the planning process needed to be approached as a comprehensive undertaking. A program would have to be customized to their local community and developed to generate local support and consensus.

Everyone who joined the planning group recognized the responsibility with which they were charged. They all agreed to examine the different strategies of the five cornerstones and work with Mayor Rose to determine how to best implement them to reach their Field of dreams.

Chapter 2: ESTABLISHING AN ECONOMIC DEVELOPMENT PROGRAM

Guiding Principles:

☞ Be public with your intentions and activities.

☞ Clearly explain to the community the need for your program and the geographic service area.

☞ Recruit reputable government and business leaders to participate in the initial organizing group.

☞ Carefully evaluate and decide on the type of organization you want to establish.

☞ Formalize the organization by filing articles of incorporation, writing bylaws, electing officers, establishing committees, and holding regular meetings.

☞ Communicate your approved economic development strategy, annual work program, budget, and successes throughout the community.

☞ Secure funding commitments to complete your annual work program.

☞ Do what you said you were going to do!

☞ Keep a long-term view. Success is achieved through small accomplishments over time.

People in the town of Field were worried. The rumors about the town's big manufacturing plant closing down had been true. Now what would the workers do? What would happen to the smaller businesses—grocers, drug stores, and cafes—if people had to move out of town to find jobs? How would the school district maintain its funding?

Fortunately, Mayor Rose was a little ahead of the game. She and other concerned citizens had organized a new economic development planning group, and their first meeting was with plant managers to find out exactly what was going on. As suspected, it was strictly a business decision, but the company wanted to work with former employees and the community as much as possible. Training was being offered for any workers who wanted to relocate to the company's newer plants, although many of them wanted to stay in Field, having lived there all their lives. So the plant managers appointed one of their supervisors, Ed, to work with the community to lessen the impact of plant closure.

Mayor Rose knew Ed, as they had grown up and graduated from high school together right there in Field. And prior to the meeting she talked to the owners of the plant and met with Ed to discuss what information was needed in order to make the meeting productive.

Ed, who started working at the plant when the original managers were still alive, had been there when the new partners took over and had seen all the incredible growth in the last few years. But when the company went public and an outside board of directors started overseeing the plant, people had become skeptical. The planning group listened intently when Ed talked about his concern for Field. His research indicated three primary sources for jobs: existing businesses could expand or diversify, new companies could start up in the community, or companies from outside the area could move in and build. He had looked at other towns similar in size to Field that had lost a primary employer.

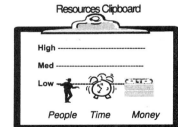

Resources Clipboard

High

Med

Low

People   Time   Money

What did successful towns do to get back on their feet? All of them had some sort of organized economic development effort.

Ed gave Mayor Rose credit for her efforts to lay the foundation for a new Field. Some people at the meeting grumbled every time he and Rose spoke of change, but most were supportive and were willing to give the Mayor and the planning group a chance.

The meeting had ended with lots of questions about what economic development really meant and what they could accomplish, so Mayor Rose decided to *organize a retreat* for the planning group. They rented a log cabin along the river managed by the Forest Service. Most of the planning group members had grown up using the cabin for day camps, sledding parties, high school dances, and potlucks. It was comfortable, and they were able to be away from phones and other interruptions.

During the morning session of the retreat, they dreamed. The facilitator called it "visioning." They thought about all the things they would like for the town. They wondered if they could find a new company to just move into the old plant and hire people back. They discussed land at the edge of town owned by the county: Could that site be used as a business park for new companies? One business owner suggested tourism as an industry, while another thought a campaign to bring in retired people would be good. Everyone was excited by the creative energy and exchange of ideas.

The facilitator suggested they put themselves in the shoes of any one of those businesses or individuals. What would someone see when they came to their town? What would make it attractive to an outside company? What did their town have to offer existing businesses and potential entrepreneurs? What did their town need? They talked about strategic planning and the need for long and short-term goals. They realized a commitment of leadership was necessary to carry out the plan once it was developed. But who was missing, and what was needed to make things happen? Who could serve as potential board members or partners with the new organization?

Over lunch, the facilitator congratulated them on their path of discovery. He pointed out that determining where you want to go always means figuring out where you're starting from.

The afternoon was spent handing out assignments. It had been an intense day, and they covered a lot of ground. They all agreed they had work to do, but it would be fun to assess their community and maybe learn something new in the process.

Why Start an Economic Development Organization?

The finest way to serve your community is to know it inside and out: the people and their livelihoods; the schools; the businesses; the churches and civic organizations; its history and landmarks; and, especially, its current economic situation. Economics is often the lifeblood of a community, and those who care about the area—who have a heartfelt desire to see it thrive and grow—will be its most ardent supporters.

The first step in an effective economic development program is creating a forum for exchanging ideas and addressing the needs of the community. This economic development organization can be structured to act as a true catalyst for growth. It will:

* *Provide a meeting place for people with common objectives.*
* *Show how unified actions are more impressive than individual endeavors.*
* *Lend legitimacy to your goals.*
* *Enable you to raise more funds.*
* *Pool resources to save time and energy.*

With power in numbers, it will be easier to spearhead changes.

ORGANIZATIONAL ACTIVITIES

Just as an entrepreneur develops a new product or creates a start-up company, your group must concentrate on the most critical factors affecting your community before establishing an economic development organization. By analyzing the opportunities, strengths, and threats, you can assess whether an economic development organization is right for the area. The steps for developing a successful organization or company are very similar, as seen below.

ACTIVITIES:	ECONOMIC DEVELOPMENT ORGANIZATION:	START-UP BUSINESS:
1 CREATE A VISION	Vision statement.	Mission statement.
2 IDENTIFY THE NEED	Is there a workforce available for new jobs?	Will people want the product?
3 DEFINE GEOGRAPHIC AREA	Will the organization be for the town, county, or region?	Is the product desired locally, regionally, or nationally?
4 IDENTIFY OTHER SERVICE GROUPS	Are we competing, coexisting, or collaborating with other organizations?	Is anyone else selling this product?
5 SECURE A WIDE RANGE OF PARTICIPANTS	Can we get the support of local groups?	Does the product add value to other products where partnerships can develop?
6 ESTABLISH A FORMAL ORGANIZATION	Public, private, or public/private partnership.	Partnership, C-corporation, S-corporation, limited liability corporation (LLC).
7 SECURE FINANCIAL COMMITMENTS	Local governments, chambers of commerce, state and federal grants, fee for service, foundations, endowments.	Savings, family, bank loans, government loans, venture capital.
8 DEVELOP A STRATEGY	Annual work plan.	Business plan.
9 HIRE PERSONNEL	Skilled employees available.	Skilled employees available.
10 IDENTIFY MEASURABLE OBJECTIVES	Jobs, tax base increase, growth.	Increased income, growth.
11 PREPARE PROGRESS REPORTS	Reports to community.	Reports to stockholders.

1 CREATING A VISION

Every community needs a vision if it wants to go
somewhere and be able to know when it has arrived.
A vision will:

> → *Guide the organization to its intended goal.*
> → → *Remind the community what it represents.*
> → → → *Inspire the people who take pride in their community.*
> → → → → *Control those unrelated activities.*
> → → → → → *Free the community of past failures.*

An excellent vision will incorporate the best of the community's history into an ideal yet feasible
view of the future. It will include an organizational charter of core values and principles, summarize
priorities, plans and goals, provide insight into the future, and identify what makes the community
unique. It will be your "declaration of interdependence" with regional activities.

From this vision you can create a **mission statement** to sum up what the organization is trying
to accomplish. It should be brief and carefully written, since it will often be used to establish its
nonprofit status. Common phrases used in economic development statements include:

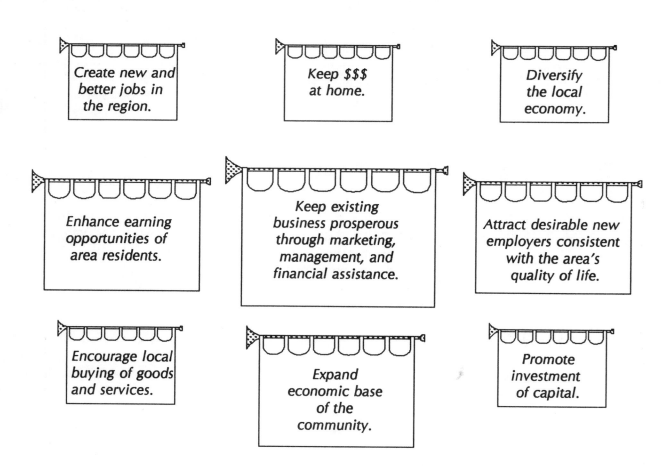

When composing a mission statement, the planning group must realize it cannot be all things to all people. Making it too generic or lofty will sound like a political slogan rather than serve as a useful blueprint for the community's future.

2 IDENTIFYING THE NEED

Before you can determine if an economic development organization is a good idea for your community, find out what the area's needs are. Too many programs are organized out of desperation, e.g., created because a primary employer shuts down a factory or moves elsewhere. The need for economic development is broader than one single action negatively impacting the community. Community leaders who are reactive rather than proactive are like a cross-eyed discus thrower: They seldom win any prizes, but sure do keep the crowd on it toes!

So, before you decide to go to the effort of organizing an economic development program. Find out:

WORKERS: *How many people are unemployed? How many are underemployed?*

STUDENTS: *How many graduate and leave town? How many drop out of school? How many are going to college and in what fields?*

BUSINESSES: *Which firms are growing in the community? What skills do they require? Which companies are having problems? What will it take to put them back on track?*

3 DEFINING THE GEOGRAPHIC SERVICE AREA

In choosing the geographic area to be served by the economic development organization, consider the following issues:

- *The larger the area, the greater the number of representatives required to fully represent all private and governmental interests.*

- *The larger the area, the greater opportunity to successfully secure private and governmental support funds.*

- *The smaller the area served, the fewer assets a community has to grow and prosper.*

A regionwide economic development organization—which increases the likelihood of a successful fund-raising campaign to assure an operating budget for part-time of full-time staffing—may be better for your community. However, there are many fine examples of successful city and village economic development programs.

4 IDENTIFYING OTHER SERVICE GROUPS

In chapter 1, we identified numerous external partners who can assist in the community's economic development effort. Chances are, a lot of existing organizations, either in the community or in the area, already perform economic development activities as part of their routine responsibilities. Most of these organizations will appreciate the focus a local comprehensive economic development organization can provide. When groups collaborate resources and energy, the entire community benefits. The trick is to avoid duplication of services and learn how to work as a team.

5 SECURING PARTICIPATION

Every successful economic development organization begins with a strong commitment by volunteers who clearly understand the need for economic development. Consequently, one of the most important steps in developing a successful program is identifying the individuals who will be responsible for setting up the formal body of the organization.

Usually, organizing committees are comprised of persons with communitywide leadership skills and name recognition. Their task is to **identify key persons to serve on the first economic development board**, such as representatives of:

- *MAJOR EMPLOYERS AND BUSINESSES*
- *SCHOOL DISTRICTS (technical schools, universities, and colleges)*
- *BANKS AND OTHER LENDING INSTITUTIONS*
- *ORGANIZED LABOR*
- *REAL ESTATE DEVELOPERS*
- *PRIVATE UTILITY REPRESENTATIVES*

- *ENVIRONMENTAL GROUPS*
- *AGRICULTURAL ORGANIZATIONS*
- *MINORITY GROUPS*
- *DOWNTOWN MERCHANTS*
- *GOVERNMENTAL DISTRICTS FOR SPECIAL SERVICES (ports, water, wastewater, and drainage districts or authorities)*

Remember, the goal is to find individuals who will apply their leadership skills to the success of the organization. Don't overlook other community activists who want to participate but do not represent one of the defined groups, as they may contribute tirelessly to the success of the organization. A group which has a sincere and enthusiastic desire to help the community is the ideal.

> ✿ SNAPSHOT ✿
>
> Smaller communities are more likely to rely on their chambers of commerce to lead efforts to strengthen the community by offering programs to attract and expand business investment.

> ✿ SNAPSHOT ✿
>
> Two-thirds of all rural communities turn to independent nonprofit entities to run their economic development program. The other third rely on local government agencies.

NOTE: an organizing committee should not include the same people who will ultimately sit on the first board of directors. Communities often include skeptics who don't fully understand the importance or need for economic development, and if the people on the organizing committee also serve on the board, they may be perceived as a clique trying to create their own power structure. If this occurs, the organization starts out with a black mark against it—which sometimes remains with them forever.

6 ESTABLISHING THE FORMAL ORGANIZATION

The type of organization your group forms will be the foundation for all its economic development activities in the future, so do not take it lightly. Carefully consider the legal requirements for a formal body, as well as the best method for securing political, business, and community participation.

WHAT TYPE OF ORGANIZATION DO YOU WANT?

When selecting the type of organization to carry out your economic development programs, remember that no one organizational model is clearly superior to another.

Your community may opt for an **economic development committee** or **task force**. In some situations, this may make sense, especially for short-term projects.

However, an **incorporated organization** usually accomplishes more economic development success because it fosters:

☆ Formal recognition by government, business and cooperative economic development organizations.

☆ Acceptance of your organization by funding sources.

☆ Formal published work program and progress evaluation.

☆ Ability to enter formal cooperative agreements.

7 SECURING FINANCIAL COMMITMENTS

Operating an economic development program costs money—lots of money, depending on the activities the community wishes to undertake. In fact, one of the most critical decisions that officers, board of directors, and members of any newly formed economic development organization need to make is the amount of funding to be raised for economic development. Funds may come from:

- $ *Local government budgets*
- $ *Chamber of commerce dues*
- $ *State and federal grants*
- $ *Business and industry grants*
- $ *Fund-raising campaigns*
- $ *Fees for provided services*
- $ *Capital endowments and foundations*
- $ *Other economic and services organizations, e.g., port authorities*

COMPARISON OF ECONOMIC DEVELOPMENT ORGANIZATIONAL MODELS

	PRIVATE	PUBLIC	PUBLIC/PRIVATE PARTNERSHIPS
Funding sources	Contributions of businesses, local industries, chambers of commerce, and individuals	Government funds (taxes); grants	Contributions of business, industry, and private individuals; grants
Governing body	Board of directors elected by membership	Mayor and city council elected by public	Elected and appointed individuals
Legal form	Nonprofit 501(c)(6) corporation	Government agency	Nonprofit 501(c)(6), (5), (4), or (3) corporation
Operational advantages	■ Not restricted by political boundaries ■ Structure allows maintenance of confidentially on important issues (e.g., identity of prospects)	■ Effective in providing development infrastructure: roads, sewer lines, water lines, etc. ■ Direct access to incentives: property tax abatement, urban development assistance grants, etc. ■ Access to policy makers	■ Not restricted by political boundaries ■ Structure allows maintenance of confidentially on important issues (e.g., identity of prospects)
Representation	Speaks effectively on business sector's interests	Speaks effectively on public sector interests	Structure allows input from all sectors of community via elected city officials
Board size	Tends to be small: 5 to 10 members	Tends to be large: 15+ members	Tends to be moderate: 7 to 13 members
Examples	■ Development corporations ■ Chambers of commerce	■ Ports ■ Local government programs	■ Economic development organizations

WHERE DO FUNDS TYPICALLY COME FROM?

Local government general funds 48%
Private sector (contributions and dues) 26%
State and federal grants 10%
Special taxes earmarked solely for economic development . 8%
Activities of the economic development organization 8%

Typically, individual board members are responsible for soliciting funds from private sector sources, while staff usually seek local, state, federal, and foundation funding assistance.

Oftentimes, the excitement of forming the organization and the promise of new jobs and investment makes the initial fund-raising easy. But it may take several years before you show visual results. Therefore, the board of directors must commit to a multi-year fund-raising effort. Attempting to complete a major fund drive every year diverts the energy of staff and the board away from program tasks needed to achieve success. Long-term (3- to 5-year) financial planning almost always pays off.

ANNUAL BUDGETS FOR ECONOMIC DEVELOPMENT:

Almost all independent nonprofit economic development organizations . . . . $100,000+
2/3rds of those organizations spend . . . . at least $250,000
Most nonprofit organizations linked to chambers of commerce . $100,000 to $1 million
15% of local government agencies spend . . . . less than $100,000
Amount rural areas should attempt to raise in order to fund an
  economic development program . . . . $3 to $6 per capita

Two broad types of funding need to be secured by the economic development organization:

- **Operational funds**, used to rent office space, pay the staff, get insurance, etc.
- **Project funds**, for specific development projects in your service territory.

Some projects of an economic development organization are labor-intensive and are paid for out of the general operating budget. Other projects may require special funding, such as capital campaigns, to generate funds over and above the operating capital of the organization.

8 DEVELOPING A STRATEGY

Like a ship captain, an economic development organization needs to chart its course and let all passengers know the destination. The new board needs to pick and choose those activities that make the best sense for the community they serve. The strategic elements of a plan are based on sound business principles and good business sense. The chapters which follow identify the various components of an economic development program.

☼ SNAPSHOTS ☼

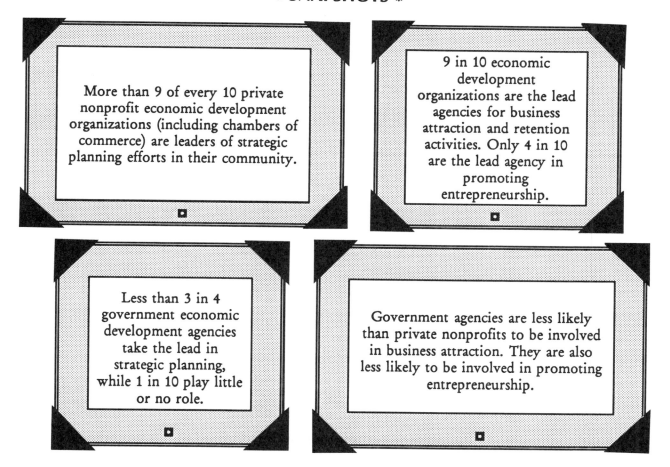

More than 9 of every 10 private nonprofit economic development organizations (including chambers of commerce) are leaders of strategic planning efforts in their community.

9 in 10 economic development organizations are the lead agencies for business attraction and retention activities. Only 4 in 10 are the lead agency in promoting entrepreneurship.

Less than 3 in 4 government economic development agencies take the lead in strategic planning, while 1 in 10 play little or no role.

Government agencies are less likely than private nonprofits to be involved in business attraction. They are also less likely to be involved in promoting entrepreneurship.

9 CREATING MEASURABLE OBJECTIVES

Because of economic conditions, resistance to public spending, and reduced budgets, communities that decide to organize an economic development program want to make sure they get their money's worth—and must be accountable to their constituents.

Economic development organizations need to communicate two types of measurements to the public: **outcomes** and **activities**.

Outcomes are quantifiable results that demonstrate the degree of success in accomplishing the objectives of the organization. Examples of outcomes are:

✓ *200 full-time employment opportunities that pay at least 175% of the national minimum wage*
✓ *$20 million in increased payrolls*
✓ *75 new indirect jobs*

✓ *$30 million in new capital investment*
✓ *$1 million in new local vendor purchases*
✓ *$1.5 million in new property taxes*
✓ *2 new food processing plants*

An economic development organization doesn't actually create the 200 new manufacturing jobs that pay at least 175% of the national minimum wage. It can, however, assist employers who create those 200 new jobs paying 175% of the national minimum wage.

Measurable **activities**, especially in smaller communities, may include such things as:

★ *Plant a tree in front of every fifth building along Main Street*
★ *Erect a new sign at the entrance on the west side of town*
★ *Select a site for a new industrial park*
★ *Partner with business and community colleges to create a workforce development committee*

★ *Create an entrepreneurial workshop for new business start-ups*
★ *Contact 30% of all existing industries for retention interviews each year*
★ *Assist 5 small businesses a week*
★ *Identify 10 community entrepreneurs each month*
★ *Find and develop 3 tourist attractions*

The economic development organization should only measure what it can control. Too many variables exist for success to be measured by outcomes alone, so by emphasizing measurable activities, the credibility of the organization will be increased. If you accomplish what you realistically promise, your long-term support in the community will be much stronger.

10 HIRING PERSONNEL

While volunteers are vital to an organization, economic development is not a part-time job or a hobby. So when a community decides to organize an economic development program, it needs qualified staff to fill the roles. Smaller communities will be able to afford only a few staff, who therefore must be able to perform most of the responsibilities.

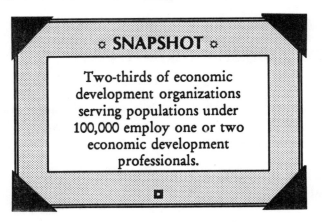

❖ **SNAPSHOT** ❖

Two-thirds of economic development organizations serving populations under 100,000 employ one or two economic development professionals.

11 MAKING PROGRESS REPORTS

Establishing an economic development organization is exciting. It captures the attention of the news media, and almost every citizen becomes involved due to the publicity and promise of the good things that will happen in the community. But as the enthusiasm for starting a new economic development organization begins to wane, and the hard work of the standing committees is not fully completed, you will need to report any progress to the community. Periodic updates help to:

— *Sustain the excitement and positive image for the future*
— *Maintain interest by funding sponsors*
— *Sustain tireless dedication of volunteers*, and
— *Complete work program objectives leading to success*

Just the Basics

In order to establish an economic development organization that has undeniable community support, the following 12 work tasks should be completed:

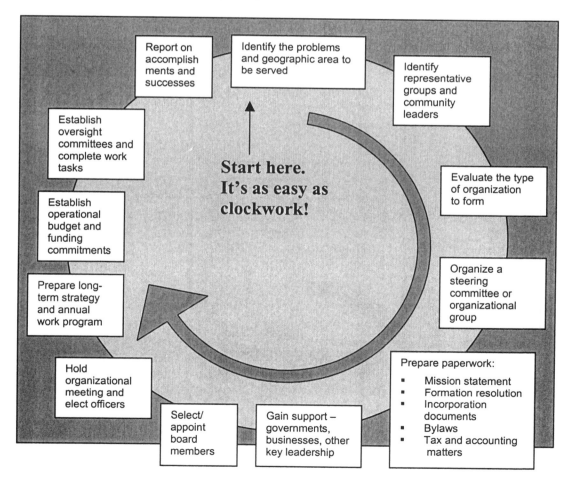

Forming an Economic Development Organization at a Glance

What can you expect to accomplish?

- ❏ Change in community image and community pride/spirit

- ❏ Increase in number of jobs in the community

- ❏ Increase in spending at and by local retail and service businesses

- ❏ Increase in population and the number of businesses in the community

Who will do the work?

- ❏ Leadership at the local or county level
- ❏ Local volunteer

- ❏ Utility company economic development representative
- ❏ Hired consultant or attorney

How will you pay for these activities?

- ❏ Fund-raising campaigns from key local supporters such as banks, utility companies, businesses
- ❏ Local government or chamber of commerce donations

- ❏ State or federal grant sources or potential partners (port authorities, planning commissions, etc.)

What role does the board member play?

- ❏ Evaluates and recommends the form of organization

- ❏ Identifies and recruits key members for board and committee assignments

- ❏ Supervises the paperwork process for incorporating the organization

- ❏ Supervises the fund-raising program and assists in gaining long-term financial support

What Success Looks Like

Well, the plant finally did close. Although it was a loss to the community, it catapulted Mayor Rose into high gear for forming her economic development organization. In a short period of time, the planning group:

✓ *Established a vision statement recognized and supported throughout the community.*

✓ *Fielded a team of volunteers who represented diverse areas of the community to serve on the board of directors and committees.*

✓ *Secured adequate and long-term financial commitments from other groups involved in the economic development activities.*

✓ *Got public recognition for presenting a well-defined organizational strategy and work plan.*

Rose knew that the economic development organization was going to be a major change in her life and the community's future. She still had lots to learn and lots of things to do before she could implement a plan and see results. However, armed with knowledge, an economic development structure, and community support, she felt confident that the decision-making process of creating new jobs for her community would be easier.

∞

REFERENCES

Bessire, Howard D. *A Handbook for the Eighties, Industrial Development.* American Economic Development Council.

Boyle, Ross, editor. *Economic Development Organization Survey Report. A Growth Strategies Organization Publication.*

Harpel, Ellen D., Deloitte & Touche Fantus Consulting Worldwide. *Guidelines for Establishing an Economic Development Organization.* The American Economic Development Council.

Kane, Matt, and Peggy Sand. *Economic Development: What Works at the Local Level.* American Economic Development Council.

Livengood, Rebecca. "Evaluating the Impact of Economic Development Programs," *Commentary,* Summer 1993.

Phillips, Phillip D., Ph.D. *Economic Development for Small Communities and Rural Areas.* University of Illinois Press.

Practicing Economic Development, third edition. AEDC Educational Foundation.

Wagner, Kenneth C. *Economic Development Manual.* American Economic Development Council.

Wagner, Kenneth C., Ph.D., and Maury Forman, Ph.D. *How to Create Jobs Now and Beyond 2000.* The Wagner Group, Brookline Massachusetts.

SECTION II.

PRODUCT DEVELOPMENT

Chapter 3:

INFRASTRUCTURE

Guiding Principles:

☞ A variety of infrastructures —water, sewer, electricity, telecommunications, roads, and others—are necessary to stimulate economic development activity.

☞ The location of businesses in the community will have a direct impact on infrastructure costs.

☞ Many infrastructures are a network of centralized and distribution facilities that can sometimes be efficiently shared with other communities.

☞ Small communities need to understand and monitor the status of all their infrastructure facilities and ensure timely capacity upgrades to meet future commercial and industrial capacity needs.

☞ Infrastructure improvements require long lead and cycle times.

☞ Availability of state-of-the-art communication networks is attractive to prospective commercial and industrial businesses.

☞ "In-place" public and private infrastructure serving commercial and industrial sites is necessary for a site to be immediately available for a relocating business.

Ed was excited about working with the new economic development planning group. He was now on a personal mission to help his former co-workers and his community. Mayor Rose had talked to him about an official type of economic development director position, and the community had just secured funding for that position. Even though it paid less than he was making at the plant, Ed agreed to work with the community and see what the future held.

The community assessment was going well. During the process of looking at the community and listening to the residents, business leaders, and elected officials, the group was learning a lot. Ed's assignment had been to assess the possibilities of having a company take over the plant that was now vacant. It was an obvious place for him to start, since he had been manager of the building for many years.

The facility was old. The sewer and water lines that serviced the building had barely been able to meet the demands of the company in the last couple of years. Work had been done on them, but when Ed talked to Public Works, their maps were confusing as to exactly where some of the lines were located. Ed met with the fire chief and learned that the building would have to be brought up to code, which meant installing a sprinkler system. When he went back to Public Works, he discovered that the current lines could not supply the additional pressure needed for a sprinkler system.

One thing seemed to lead to another. The municipal sewage treatment plant manager told him that the treatment plant was currently at 80 percent capacity and upgrades would have to be made soon to keep up with any kind of growth. The City Council was looking at growth projections for their long-range capital facilities planning.

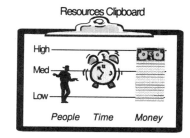

Resources Clipboard

Fortunately, news from the power company was more encouraging. Don, one of the community planning group members, was the community liaison for the power company. Don worked with Ed to gather information. The power company could easily supply electricity for any anticipated growth in the community.

The phone company had both good and bad news regarding advanced data transmission and communication technologies. It first assured Ed that the phone company could install any number of phone lines needed. The entire area would be getting fiber optics installation, but it wasn't scheduled for two to three years.

The land itself also was filled with mixed blessings. The site was environmentally clean. Ed knew from when he worked at the plant that every time the owners had explored plant expansion with the bank, federal flood insurance coverage had been an issue. The back property line bordered a federally designated flood plain along the river. That parcel had flooded sometimes in the spring, but it had never bothered the plant because nothing was built there. Now, the town had to resolve whether that whole area was in or out of the flood plain. And then there were new environmental rules about stormwater run-off drainage—a whole story in itself.

Ed realized that before the plant could reopen, a great deal of work needed to be done. All of this work was going to cost money. He had no idea if investing in the plant would even be worth it. And who would pay for it? Investing in upgrading the plant would mean putting all the community's hopes in this building. Would the infrastructure improvements help other parts of the community as well, so that they could have other options for job creation?

Ed was discovering that infrastructure was a complicated, interwoven issue that involved many agencies, lots of money, and much long-term planning.

What is Infrastructure?

Infrastructure is the physical support system needed for the delivery of goods and services. It includes water and sewer pipes, roads, bridges, cables, telecommunications, power, water, and sewage treatment plants. Capacity of infrastructure refers to the measure of what the infrastructure is able to do: How many cars can cross the bridge per hour? How fast can data flow in a fiber optic cable? How many gallons of sewage can be treated per day?

Both government and private businesses provide infrastructure. Public infrastructure usually includes water, wastewater, and stormwater systems; streets and road improvements; as well as schools, hospitals, and other public services. Private infrastructure includes natural gas and electric distribution, and telephone and telecommunications systems. although these services are sometimes provided by the public sector or cooperative associations.

Planning for economic development occurs within the context of ongoing capital improvement planning that jurisdictions are required to do, so it is important to continually coordinate infrastructure planning with local officials. The construction of infrastructure usually requires capital outlays and the use of debt financing, which is repaid from user rates and charges and tax revenues.

INFRASTRUCTURE BASICS

INFRASTRUCTURE TYPE	TYPICAL SUPPLIER	DISTRIBUTION FACILITIES	CENTRAL FACILITIES	INTER-REGIONAL NETWORK	NETWORK TO BUSINESS
WATER SUPPLY	Government	Pipes	Purification reservoirs, storage tanks	Possibly	Yes
SANITARY SEWER	Government	Pipes	Treatment	No	Yes
STORMWATER DRAINAGE	Government	Pipes	No	No	Yes
FLOOD CONTROL	Government	Channels	Possibly	Possibly	No
ELECTRIC POWER	Business or government	Cables, substations	Generation	Yes	Yes
NATURAL GAS	Business	Pipes	Storage tanks	Yes	Yes
SOLID WASTE DISPOSAL	Government or business	Dumpsters, transfer stations	Landfills, incinerators	Possibly	No
ROADS AND BRIDGES	Government	Roads and bridges	Maintenance yards	Yes	Yes
AIRPORTS	Government	Airspace buffer zones	Runways, terminals	Yes	No
RAILROADS	Business	Tracks and connecting roads and ports	Yards, maintenance	Yes	Yes
PORTS AND DOCKS	Government	Canals and locks	Docks and dockside	Possibly	No
WIRELINE TELE-COMMUNICATIONS	Business	Cables	Switches, long-distance points	Yes	Yes
WIRELESS TELE-COMMUNICATIONS	Business	Antenna towers	No	Yes	Yes

Why is Infrastructure Investment Important?

Infrastructure investment provides capital for water, waste removal, energy, transportation, telecommunications, and the other services and facilities necessary to retain and expand existing business and incubate or attract new business. Many industries have special infrastructure requirements because of the types of processes used in their particular businesses. The benefits of infrastructure investment are:

Supports Existing Businesses	Provides necessary services and promotes retention and expansion.
Increases Productivity	Higher quality of existing infrastructure often leads to more efficient production.
Improves Quality of Life	Increased quality of infrastructure makes the community more livable for workers and retirees.
Enhances Negotiation	Inclusion as part of an overall package of incentives will attract industries.
Facilitates Economic Development	Infrastructure is often identified as the number one or two issue for community prosperity.
Prompts a Domino Effect	Properly laid out roads, water, sewer, telecommunications, and powerlines will lead to better buildings and local services.
Links Regions	Connects citizens in one community to other communities and outside opportunities.
Satisfies Health Requirements	Fulfills our biological needs of safe drinking water and disposing of waste.
Stabilizes Rates and Taxes	Routine investments minimize future costs.
Achieves Competitive Advantage	Makes your community attractive to relocating businesses.
Assists in Economic Diversification	Upgrading infrastructure leads to more diverse business clientele.

One goal of an economic development organization is to help local government officials understand why it is important to develop communitywide utility systems that will have the capacity to service the needs of existing businesses as well as additional businesses or residents in the future. The organization should also work with private utility companies to anticipate the growth and to invest in state-of-the-art services—especially communication systems and material disposal requirements—for the industries being recruited for the community. Companies that will benefit from infrastructure improvements may be willing to pay a portion of the construction costs if their operating costs will be reduced. Therefore, the community should have development regulations and fees in place before companies apply for building permits.

Some states require communities to predetermine how much public support will be provided and how it will be paid for. For example, under Washington State's Growth Management Act, communities must establish "level of service standards" and maintain "concurrency" with those levels of service.

Economic development organizations typically have little direct say in how infrastructure investments are made. Those decisions are usually left to local government or governmental utility suppliers and private businesses who plan, construct, maintain, and pay for infrastructure. In Washington State, however, the passage of the Grange Power Act gave rural communities the ability to form nonprofit community-operated utility districts (PUDs). The PUDs succeeded in bringing electricity to farms and small towns throughout the state. Now, with many companies requiring additional infrastructure investment, the PUDs will need increased authority to assist communities that don't want to be left behind or unable to compete.

CHARACTERISTICS OF INFRASTRUCTURE INVESTMENT

VERY EXPENSIVE

To plan, engineer, and construct infrastructure improvement is often very costly relative to current budgets.

MULTI-COMMUNITY COOPERATION PAYS

Nearby communities that share infrastructure systems lessen the financial drain on their citizens who would otherwise have to pay for separate systems.

STATE AND FEDERAL FUNDING SOURCES AVAILABLE

Various forms of government assistance and intergovernmental agreements can reduce the reliance on tax and user fee increases.

REQUIRES AGGRESSIVE, CREATIVE FINANCING TOOLS

Most communities will need to obtain special financing, including state and federal grant and loan programs and local fees. Private utilities may want guarantees of future usage in order to make investments.

VOTERS AND ECONOMIC DEVELOPMENT BOARDS ONLY INFLUENCE, NOT DECIDE

Local government officials (or governmental utility suppliers) and private businesses that plan, construct, maintain, and pay for infrastructure ultimately call the shots.

TAX AND USER FEE INCREASES

Speculatively expanding a system may require increased charges to existing users until new users start to buy service. Rural communities that charge below-market user fees may be required to increase rates to become eligible for state and federal assistance programs.

LOCATION- AND USER-DRIVEN

Costs of infrastructure improvements depend upon where and to whom services will be provided. If networks need to be extended over great distances and to larger numbers of users, costs of improvements will rise.

KEY QUESTIONS ABOUT INFRASTRUCTURE

The economic development organization will need to coordinate with local government officials and private utility representatives to assure that upgraded services are planned for commercial and industrial areas and that the improvement schedule matches the time line of the economic development strategy. So before any state-of-the-art infrastructure is agreed upon, the economic development organization must encourage a cautious approach by advocating the right amount and type of infrastructure, as well as reasonable costs for operating a business. Keep the following in mind as you deal with experts:

1. Will the benefits of having this improved infrastructure be worth the costs to the community?

2. Would having this particular infrastructure in place before there are customers to use it make our community sufficiently more attractive to new businesses?

3. What are the risks in waiting to build this infrastructure? What are the risks in moving forward now?

4. Will the increased taxes or user charges for this upgraded infrastructure hurt existing businesses? If so, how much?

5. Are there other ways to solve the problem other than developing new infrastructure?

6. How else can we pay for this infrastructure other than what has been proposed?

7. Is the infrastructure at this site going to be balanced? For example, if there is no way to get water to the site, is there any point in installing electric lines?

8. Can our community take advantage of existing infrastructure in nearby communities?

9. Would sharing facilities with other communities reduce the costs of this infrastructure?

10. What could we gain by having this infrastructure plan verified by someone outside of our community?

11. How else could we beneficially spend our money for economic development than having this infrastructure?

12. Have we asked managers in the kinds of businesses we desire to tell us what their infrastructure requirements are?

13. How might the infrastructure being proposed for this site be extended efficiently to serve other sites?

14. Is this particular infrastructure consistent with our economic development strategy?

15. As long as we are digging a trench for one kind of infrastructure (cables, water mains), can any other kind of infrastructure be placed in the trench at the same time?

16. What is the budget for all of the operating and maintenance costs that this new infrastructure will generate?

17. Do any pending regulatory changes make our infrastructure plans potentially more risky or more costly?

18. Can we support any regulatory or legislative changes to help our community get the infrastructure we need sooner?

19. What technology alternatives have been considered in this infrastructure proposal?

20. What are the rates for this kind of utility service in communities with whom we compete or compare?

CAUSES OF CONCERN

Despite all the good intentions that improved infrastructure may bring to a community, there is potential for disaster if the development is not thought out carefully. The following situations could cause businesses to fail or leave:

- ⊗ *Poor location*
- ⊗ *Short life span*
- ⊗ *Inadequate capacity*
- ⊗ *Excessive regulatory requirements*
- ⊗ *Inconsistent reliability*
- ⊗ *Community risks in failure modes (e.g., contamination, economic disruption)*

- ⊗ *Environmental impacts (noise, smell, etc.)*
- ⊗ *Durability and maintenance requirements*
- ⊗ *Inability to upgrade or expand*
- ⊗ *Costly government-imposed fees and taxes*
- ⊗ *Inability to recover capital costs*
- ⊗ *Inability to recover operating costs*

Just the Basics

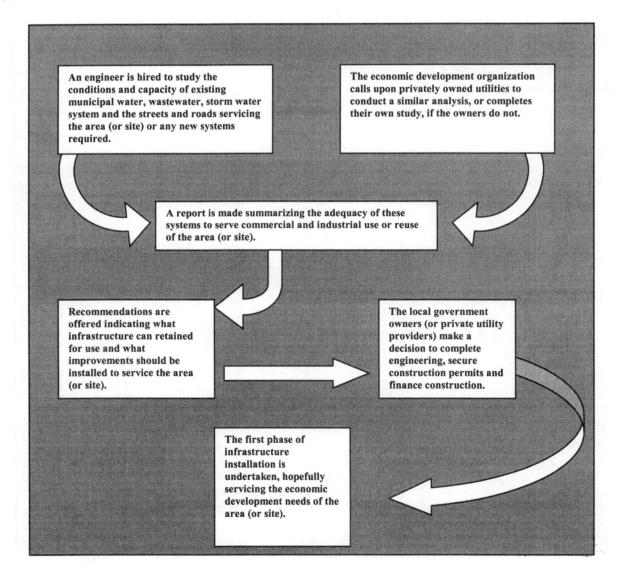

INFRASTRUCTURE ACTIVITIES

STRATEGY	KEEP UP / CATCH UP	BUILD ON WHAT YOU HAVE	BUILD UPON REQUEST	IF YOU BUILD IT, THEY WILL COME
DEFINITION	Make improvements and repairs to existing infrastructure to meet existing needs and standards.	Add capacity to existing infrastructure to allow expansion.	Actively build new infrastructure with excess capacity as a way to attract businesses.	Speculatively build new infrastructure with excess capacity as a way to attract businesses.
WHEN TO USE	• Business retention • Population increases • Lack of prior maintenance	• Growth businesses • Existing businesses willing to share costs	• Business attraction • Part of incentive package	• Change in development direction
RISK	Balanced by the possibility that existing businesses may leave.	Varies depending on business's commitment to stay in community.	Moderate	High
PRACTICAL TIPS	▶ Conduct a pollution prevention audit. ▶ Optimize existing system operations. ▶ Implement conservation load reduction program.	▶ Share costs between public and private partners. ▶ Ensure that facilities are expandable.	▶ Determine if company facilities are too specialized and irrelevant to other industries. ▶ Check development needs with development ordinances. ▶ Quantify community tradeoffs.	▶ Base design on demonstrated needs. ▶ Develop facility conversion plan in case attraction efforts fail.
NORTHWEST EXAMPLES	Weyerhaeuser takes care of inflow and infiltration in Raymond, WA.	Port of Willapa Harbor, WA, and Natural Biopolymer.	Disney, Intel, Weyerhaeuser, BHP.	Ports of Chehalis and Centralia, WA, built an industrial park with no initial customers or prospects.

THE MASTER PLAN

Infrastructure investment requires a carefully prepared master plan—including a land use plan and capital improvement program—to show where and when public and private infrastructure will be required to service existing and future commercial and industrial users.

The consultants who prepare a master plan should provide a document that answers the following questions:

1. What infrastructure do we need to install?

2. Who is responsible for its installation?

3. How much will it cost?

4. How can it be paid for—by fees, taxes, or grants?

5. Can it be financed over several years?

6. What is the financial impact to existing users, taxpayers, and/or shareholders?

7. How long will it take to design, engineer, secure construction permits, and complete the improvements?

8. Can the improvements be phased and scheduled over several years, if portions will be for speculative economic development?

9. What is the earliest planned "tap-in" date for each portion of the commercial or industrial areas (or site) to be serviced?

10. Can it be expanded?

Infrastructure at a Glance

What can you expect to accomplish?

- ❑ The ability to provide a fully serviced commercial or industrial site to a prospective business

- ❑ Detailed, site-specific plans that show type of infrastructure improvements necessary at sites, time lines of development, and costs

- ❑ Backup strategies for seeking infrastructure investments from alternative providers

- ❑ A master utility services plan for the community

- ❑ Identification of costs necessary to provide needed utilities to various portions of the community

- ❑ Documented assurances of coordinated investment by private utilities for services such as electricity, gas, and telecommunications

Who will do the work?

- ❑ Existing public works personnel

- ❑ Engineering consultant

- ❑ Private utility staff

Who will pay for these activities?

- ❑ Local government

- ❑ Businesses that will benefit

- ❑ State and/or federal grants and loans

- ❑ Private utilities making investments that will yield additional user revenues from present and future customers

What role does the board member play?

- ❑ Assists in securing funding for the study

- ❑ Supervises study for commercial and industrial areas of concern

- ❑ Asks smart, challenging questions of the experts

- ❑ Maintains a balanced focus on costs, benefits, risks, and alternatives

What Success Looks Like

Ed and Don, with support from other members of Field's economic development planning group, convinced the leadership of their community to fund an infrastructure assessment and improvement plan. They identified the shortcomings and adequacies of the community's infrastructure capacity, then prioritized the critical issues and determined the best actions to take to achieve their goals. The process helped to clarify the importance of infrastructure improvements and elevated it on the community's priority list.

Ed proudly reported the results of this study:

✓ *A state grant was received and a bond was approved to fund the first phase of construction, which will provide capacity and supply lines to the old plant and surrounding industrial park sites.*

✓ *A floodplain management study and a stormwater drainage plan are being prepared by an engineer.*

✓ *Streets, roads, and sidewalks will be improved, along with sewers, wastewater treatment plants, and storage tanks.*

✓ *Field will have a fully serviced site on which to construct a new building.*

✓ *The community has assurances from private utilities who will design and install electric, gas, and communication services during the building construction phase so when the building is done there will be no delay in making the site available.*

The plan integrates well with the economic development organization's goals of having at least one site (if not two) ready for immediate occupancy by a business at all times. Ed knows that his community is going to be appealing to potential prospects. And the community now realizes that development happens only when residential, industrial, and commercial interests are working together.

∞

REFERENCES

Bevard, Joseph H. *Capital Facilities Planning*. APA Planners Press, American Planning Association.

Infrastructure Financing for Small Communities in Washington State. Washington State Community, Trade and Economic Development, Olympia, WA, 1999.

Infrastructure Support for Economic Development. Planning Advisory Service, American Planning Association.

Johnson, Steve. "Rural PUDs Can Plug You In," *Seattle Times*, February 16, 1999.

Planning, Growth, and Public Facilities. Planners Advisory Service, American Planning Association.

Chapter 4

GATEWAY PROGRAMS

Guiding Principles:

☞ Identify and map the physical attributes that give character to your community.

☞ Develop a capacity for broad based civic responsibility.

☞ Start off small and grow into larger efforts as additional time and money are identified.

☞ Create an image and communicate that image to passers-by!

☞ Go beyond the regulations to protect resources and ensure quality development.

☞ Maintain and update activities as seasons change.

☞ Identify sponsors who can be responsible for specific areas of the community.

☞ Design outcomes that capture the attention of the viewer.

☞ Set standards for future use, and define a community's vision and values.

☞ Cultivate responsible developers.

Noel owned a small printing company in Field. He had moved to town 15 years ago, and his printing business had grown from being in his basement to a small storefront downtown. He employed two others and had just added some computerized equipment that would enable him to take on more complex jobs. But Noel was worried about the future now that the plant had closed. He knew there would be less money circulating in the community.

Noel was happy that Rose had asked him to be a part of the Economic Development Planning Group. It seemed as if the small business owners were often excluded from meetings such as these, that too often decisions were made by a handful of people who ignored the businesses in town. As a downtown merchant, he was aware of the failed efforts to "perk up" downtown, yet was trying to look at his town with "new eyes," as the retreat facilitator had suggested.

Now Noel and his family were on their way back from a camping trip along the river. He had enjoyed the time away from the business, and the fishing had been good. He appreciated being so close to a scenic and recreational area.

As they approached the outskirts of town, Noel was suddenly uncomfortable with what he saw. The sign at the outskirts was faded, with one corner broken, and he noticed that the population number was at least ten years out of date. Another sign nearby promoted the town as being "Most Beautiful City, 1983." Underneath that sign were overgrown weeds and broken bottles. Trash littered the entire area. The privately-owned property on the other side of the road had buildings that were nearly falling down.

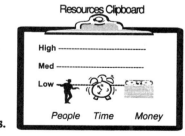

Why hadn't Noel ever noticed this before? He passed this way many times. Maybe the entire community had become numb to these eyesores. Was this the impression they wanted to give to visitors who came to town? Would people even want to stop and eat, let alone shop or consider moving here, after seeing the entryway? Noel was certainly not proud of that entrance to his town. What a shame, he thought, it had taken his participation with the planning group to really see his town with "new eyes." He made a mental note to mobilize a group to clean up the mess.

What are Gateways?

The gateways of a community are usually the roads and highways leading from the edge of a town or neighborhood into a central business district. They are also the routes leading from other portals of entry, such as by air, rail, or sea.

Gateway programs are designed to enhance the entrance ways to give the viewer a positive image of the community and encourage appropriate types of development. The programs may include image-building physical improvement activities as well as land use controls. These two major components are intended for both short- and long-term projects.

Why is a Gateway Program Important?

Builds Positive Image	It shows a community's healthy face to visitors and residents. It makes a statement on how the community feels about itself.
Enhances Transportation	It protects major transportation corridors from lower standards of development.
Promotes Community Pride	It provides an opportunity for communitywide projects.
Enhances Community Design Theme	It promotes a concept to make the community unique and able to distinguish itself to visitors and prospects.

CHARACTERISTICS OF GATEWAY PROGRAMS

PROJECTS CAN BE SHORT- or LONG-TERM

Projects are normally short-term in scope; however, it may involve long-term maintenance concerning the elements of the image, sign, or landscaping.

PROVIDES LONG-TERM GUIDANCE

Land use controls are usually developed with a vision of a community's future.

VISUALLY APPEALING

Results can be physically seen rather than quantifiably justified.

COMMUNITY BUY-IN

Land use controls are usually included in a comprehensive plan which requires formal adoption by community.

MINIMAL OPPOSITION

It is hard to oppose gateway projects that enhance a community's appearance and are low-cost.

CUSTOMIZED TO COMMUNITY RESOURCES

Projects do not need to be expensive in order to enhance the community image. They may be as elaborate as they are affordable.

ACCOMPLISHED WITH VOLUNTEER LABOR

Many community beautification projects can be completed using volunteers. Often, sponsoring organizations will come forward to help with time, money, and energy.

Gateway Activities

Each of the two major categories—physical improvements and land use controls—has many subcomponents that determine the community's ultimate success or failure. Success is directly proportionate to the degree of understanding and commitment to each.

Physical Improvements

The first method of improving the gateway is conducting an analysis of what the community looks like and implementing a plan to enhance its appearance. Each assessment is community-specific, so consider the following as you walk and drive around town with a scrutinizing, unapologetic attitude:

- ▶ *Is signage clean, crisp, and readable?*
- ▶ *Are billboards tastefully placed, or do they clutter the roadway?*
- ▶ *Are sidewalks in walkable condition and well-lit?*
- ▶ *Is graffiti scrawled all over the walls of vacant buildings?*
- ▶ *Do road signs direct visitors to information centers or kiosks?*

Just the Basics

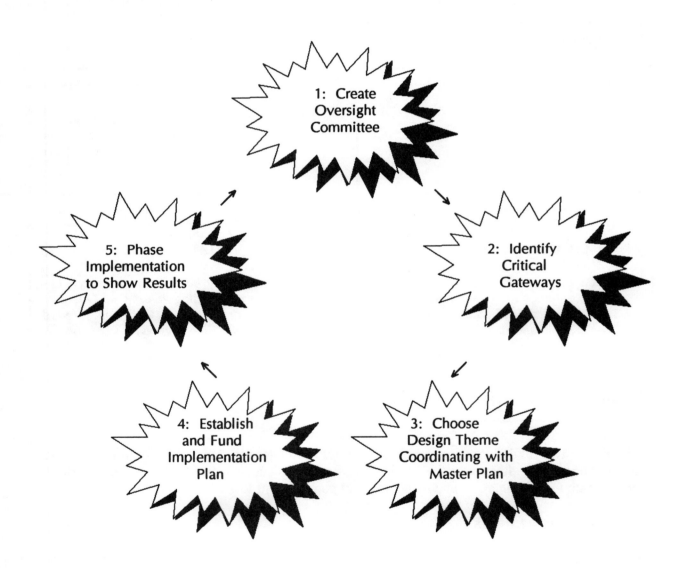

PHYSICAL IMPROVEMENT
STRATEGIES FOR CREATING YOUR GATEWAY

ADOPT AN OVERALL COMMUNITY THEME. Consider a design that reflects a certain era, such as Baker City, Oregon, and its Victorian turn-of-the-century architecture, or a specific cultural theme, such as Leavenworth, Washington's highly successful Bavarian-style architecture along its gateway corridor.

PLANT MORE INTENSIVE AMOUNTS OF TREES AND GROUND COVER, including plants that require higher-than-normal maintenance, thus insuring routine landscaping.

INSTALL:

◇ Brick paver stones instead of concrete sidewalks.

◇ Decorative trash receptacles, sitting benches, flower pots/vaults.

◇ Pedestrian information/location signs.

◇ Decorative street and traffic signs.

◇ Uniform property information and address signs.

◇ Decorative lighting rather than the standard utility lighting poles and elevated illumination.

✿ **SNAPSHOT** ✿

The basic unit of planning is the neighborhood.
A neighborhood standing alone is a hamlet or village.
A cluster of neighborhoods becomes a town.
Clusters of many neighborhoods become a community.

Land Use Controls

Once you have envisioned how the entryway of your community will look, take steps to maintain standards so that responsible growth can occur without negatively affecting the neighborhoods.

First, find out what your community's current zoning, growth, and land use policies and regulations are. In some areas, growth management legislation may prohibit or encourage the types of activities your economic development organization wants to undertake. Take this opportunity to establish a rapport with clerks or officials of local, county, and state government licensing and regulatory agencies to learn as much as you can about what can and cannot be done.

By utilizing land use controls, gateways and neighborhoods will be protected and enhanced while the existing businesses are allowed to continue with their trades. Altering the physical appearance of the landscape does not come without cost, so implementing the following strategies prior to development is the best and least costly way to accomplish your goals. The sooner these land use controls are put in place, the better.

LAND USE CONTROL
STRATEGIES FOR CREATING YOUR GATEWAY

DEVELOP A COMPREHENSIVE PLAN — Create a formal planning document that provides a framework for local land use decisions based on a community's values and vision for the future.

ESTABLISH ZONING — Zoning defines the allowable uses for specified areas, such as gateways, and enables a community to avoid incompatible adjacent uses.

ENCOURAGE A TRANSFER OF DEVELOPMENT RIGHTS — This transfer will protect valued areas of the community at little or no cost to the community by concentrating development away from designated areas, such as a gateway.

DEMAND CONDITIONS, COVENANTS, AND RESTRICTIONS — These rules may insist on design standards, construction standards, signage, and lighting stipulations that will enhance and maintain a point of entry.

CHOOSE CLUSTER DEVELOPMENT — This is intended to protect some areas of land by requiring that development be concentrated on a specified suitable area. Gateways can be considered as undeveloped areas, whereas the land around it may be used more productively while maintaining a suitable entryway.

THINK ABOUT INFILL — For communities that want to maintain prime rural lands leading into their community, infilling steers development toward existing facilities and vacant lots near the community's core areas.

DEVELOP OVERLAY ZONING — For communities that have not included a gateway clause in their established zoning ordinance, this classification creates an additional set of land use requirements that are specific to an overlay district, such as a gateway.

❖ SNAPSHOT ❖

Rural communities often have relaxed or absent land use policies for undeveloped land adjacent to a gateway or living area.
In some towns, however, farmland preservation is of paramount importance, and local or regional land use policies may have recently been enacted to prevent fertile fields from becoming shopping centers and parking lots.

GATEWAY DEVELOPMENT PLAN

Activity	Description	Champion	Budget	Start Date	End Date
Concept	The concept of gateways and their importance is sold to the community.				
	Measurement: The community is talking about the importance of the gateways and their impact on the community.				
Committee Development	A gateway committee is formed to create a gateway plan.				
	Measurement: Discussion is increasing in the public arena.				
Community Input Solicited	The committee holds a number of public meetings to receive citizen input on the needs of gateway improvements.				
	Measurement: The committee has ensured that citizen input into the plan is achieved.				
Plan Development	The gateway committee develops its plans through internal assessment, reviewing other projects, and professional assistance, if necessary.				
	Measurement: Gateway plan is drafted and completed.				
Public Review	Citizen hearings are conducted to allow for review of the gateway improvement plan.				
	Measurement: Public review and comment is received.				
Plan Revision	Based on citizen comments, the gateway plan would be amended to reflect community input.				
	Measurement: The gateway committee revises the plan to accommodate community opinions.				
Gateway Plan adopted by the Planning Commission	Gateway plan is submitted to the Planning Commission for review.				
	Measurement: Planning Commission adopts plan.				
Gateway Plan adopted by the Town Council	Gateway plan is submitted to the Town Council for review.				
	Measurement: Town Council adopts plan.				
Funding	Funding for specific projects identified in the plan is secured.				
	Measurement: The money is in the bank.				
Implementation	Projects are implemented as a result of this planning effort.				
	Measurement: The plan is implemented.				

Gateway Programs at a Glance

What can you expect to accomplish?

- ❑ A concise description of the image of the community
- ❑ Consensus on how to beautify the entrance to the community

- ❑ Creation of a positive first impression for visitors and residents
- ❑ A theme that describes the community to people passing through

- ❑ Compatible uses of adjacent land

Who will do the work?

- ❑ Students as part of class projects
- ❑ Chamber of commerce or a committee of the chamber

- ❑ Committee of the economic development organization
- ❑ Separate body—possibly a combination of public and private interests

- ❑ Volunteers from non-profit organizations
- ❑ Local government planning commission

How will you pay for these activities?

- ❑ In-kind volunteer activities
- ❑ Private donations or other funds

- ❑ Sponsors
- ❑ Fundraisers

- ❑ Local government funds
- ❑ State and/or federal support

What role does the board member play?

- ❑ Assists in preparing the plan
- ❑ Serves as a construction volunteer, if applicable

- ❑ Assists in identifying and securing funding

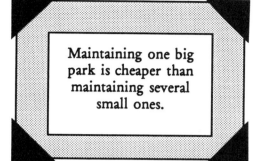

> Maintaining one big park is cheaper than maintaining several small ones.

> The size of a neighborhood is usually defined as a 5-minute walking distance (or 1/4 mile) from the edge to the center and a 10-minute walk edge to edge.

What Success Looks Like

Noel was very pleased. The shoddy sign at the entrance way to Field had been replaced with a new sign using the "Logging Era" design theme they adopted. Flowers at its base and lighting reflected the pride the community now felt. New planters were added along the entrance corridor, and a tree planting program to create an arboretum along the gateways into town had begun.

As a spinoff from the gateway planning effort, the community also developed a "Lumber Days" festival. Visitors from five states came to Field for the celebration. The gateway program really put Noel's town on the map, and he felt proud of the accomplishments.

More importantly, Mayor Rose had worked with the city council to develop a comprehensive plan that provided a framework for local land use. They had also instructed the planning office to review zoning regulations and established a plan to avoid incompatible adjacent uses.

REFERENCES

Abbott, Sue, and Sally Sheridan. *Building Gateway Partnerships: A Process for Shaping the Future of Your Community (Training Workbook)*. Lowe Enterprises, Inc., and the American Planning Association, April 1997.

Bradford, Susan. "Design Guidelines, How to Make Them Work for You," *Builder Magazine*, May 1994.

Brown-Manrique, Gerardo, "Design Guidelines as Controls on Development," *Small Town*, May-June 1991.

Glassford, Peggy. *Appearance Codes for Small Communities*. American Planning Association.

Mandelker, Daniel R., and William R. Ewald. *Street Graphics*. APA Planners Press.

"7 Secrets to Coping with Change in Small Towns," *Northwest Strategy Community Development Guide*, USDA Forest Service, 1990.

Chapter 5:

DOWNTOWN REVITALIZATION

Ed had a luncheon date with Andrea, a member of the economic planning group and new Forest Service supervisor for their district. She wanted to know a little more about the area, and Ed offered to show her his hometown and tell about its 150-year history.

As they walked along Main Street in Field, Ed pointed out some of the vacant storefronts that lined the sidewalk. "This is where Pop's Department Store and the Family Pharmacy used to be," he said. "And over there were the diner and candy store."

"What was in that big old brick building on the corner?" Andrea asked.

"Well, the second and third floors were doctors' and dentists' offices, and the main floor was the post office," Ed said. "They've all moved into new buildings out on the main stretch of roadway coming into town." It seemed that almost all of the businesses Ed used to frequent as a kid were gone. Now, second-hand stores, dingy and dilapidated buildings, and boarded-up storefronts occupied much of Main Street.

"I can see why they'd want to move," Andrea said. "There doesn't appear to be much life down here."

As he and Andrea sat down in a booth at Betty's Cafe—the only place downtown that served lunch—Ed lamented, "Downtown used to be the center of civic and social activity in Field, as well as *the* place to shop. And they just don't make buildings anymore that have such character. Downtown really symbolized the community's identity and embodied our rich heritage."

"Why do some of the buildings look so tacky now?" Andrea asked.

"Well," Ed explained, "about ten years ago, downtown business owners tried to halt the spiraling economic decline by emulating the competition in some suburban areas. They slip-covered buildings with aluminum, plywood, and multi-colored tile, then tacked garish, oversized signs to upper-story facades. Instead of improving downtown's appearance or economic stability, these well-meaning but misguided efforts merely blurred the distinction between downtown and competing areas. In trying to save downtown, its merchants masked the qualities that had made it unique."

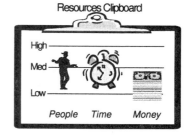

Andrea understood his concerns. She knew that citizens, government officials, and business leaders all over the country were mourning the demise of their traditional and historic core. Competition from shopping malls, "big box" retailers, mail-order services, and the Internet, as well as changes in consumer shopping patterns, had resulted in the deterioration of many older commercial business districts. Suburban industrial parks with newer buildings and more convenient transportation access had also encouraged many manufacturing and industrial businesses to relocate out of downtown.

Andrea told Ed about the successful Main Street Program where she had lived before. "The planners got the entire community involved, and they took a long-range, comprehensive approach. Within a few years, the downtown became a thriving center for that area." She also told him about other communities and their strategies for putting fresh energy into their downtowns.

As Ed walked back to his office, he no longer saw empty downtown storefronts. Instead he imagined the core area being brought back to life by preservation-minded investors and shoppers looking for something other than strip malls and warehouse discount chains. He saw buildings put back into productive use. He wondered if city officials could be convinced that downtown was worth reinvesting in. Ed knew something needed to be done soon to turn the spiral around, before the heart and soul of his community would be gone forever.

What is Downtown Revitalization?

Downtown revitalization is enhancing the social, political, physical, and economic value of the traditional central business district of a community. The goal is to expand and improve the livability and sustainability of the entire community by attracting employment, shopping, recreation, and social activities.

The most recognizable and basic downtown revitalization activities include:

♦ *Organizing a body of people who have a special interest in the district.*

♦ *Preparing a design plan for land use and physical appearance improvements for both privately and publicly owned property.*

♦ *Devising a strategy to restructure the downtown retail, commercial, and light industrial economy, including strategic business recruitment programs.*

♦ *Sponsoring special events to increase visitor and customer traffic in the downtown, as well as celebrations in the district.*

Successful downtown revitalization requires a carefully organized plan, long-term financial commitments, and cooperation from property owners, business owners, local government officials, and residents of the community. A comprehensive revitalization program—due to the high levels of time, money, and individual involvement required—are not for the faint of heart. However, from a community investment standpoint, it offers a greater chance for quick success than many other forms of economic development undertaken in a small community.

Why is Downtown Revitalization Important?

Improves Image	Downtown is often what gives visitors their first impressions of a community.
Makes Use of Existing Buildings	Assists communities in managing growth through reuse of property.
Develops a Sense of Community	Provides central location for community-wide projects.
Provides Variety of Retail Options	The more stores there are in an area, the more people will gather and shop.
Prevents Blight and Abandonment	Reduces health and safety costs and concerns; discourages vagrancy and vandalism.
Perpetuates Community Character and History	Visible signs of the past can be retained and stories can be passed on to the next generation.
Encourages New and Complementary Businesses	Businesses want to be where people are and money is being spent, so it strengthens an existing business cluster.
Expands the Tax Base	Generates local revenues to pay for community services.
Increases Employment Opportunities	Replaces jobs lost through natural attrition and encourages entrepreneurs.
Regains Status as Central Shopping District	Pulls in shoppers from a radius beyond the city limits.
Plugs Leakage of Dollars	Citizens will no longer need to shop at retail businesses outside of the community.

❖ SNAPSHOT ❖

An empty downtown commercial building costs the local economy $40 in lost economic activity for every dollar in rent lost to the property owner.

◾

CHARACTERISTICS OF REVITALIZATION PROGRAMS

EXPENSES SUITED TO BUDGET

Downtown revitalization projects and activities, whether improvements in appearance or advertising and promotion, can be undertaken at different levels of expense depending on available funds.

PEOPLE-INTENSIVE

Most efforts will require consensus, cooperation, and coordination from a large number of people including volunteers.

REQUIRES PUBLIC AND PRIVATE PARTNERSHIPS

True cooperation between the public and private sector must be achieved in all activities, including financial support.

LONG-TERM GOALS

Significant changes to a downtown will require more time, so results will not be immediately evident.

WIDE RANGE OF ACTIVITIES

An unlimited number of projects and activities, large and small, can help revitalize a downtown.

BETTER INVESTMENT RATIO

From a community investment standpoint, this economic development approach provides a greater source of return than other strategies.

INCREASED REVENUE FROM OUTSIDE SPENDING

Festivals and special events in the downtown area bring outside dollars into a community.

What is the Main Street Approach™?

In 1977, the National Trust for Historic Preservation, concerned about continuing threats to downtown's commercial architecture, launched a pilot program to stimulate economic activity in small-city downtowns. This program ultimately helped develop a comprehensive downtown revitalization strategy to encourage economic development within the context of historic preservation. Today, this very successful strategy, known as the Main Street Approach™, has been implemented in more than 1,400 towns and cities throughout 41 of the United States.

The intent of a Main Street Approach™ program is to complete a prescribed set of actions and activities designed to improve the economic well-being of a traditional commercial business district and employment center within a community. Main Street Approach™ focuses on four points: **organization, promotion, design**, and **economic restructuring**. All four activities must be integrated for a successful downtown strategy to take place. Each activity reinforces the other three.

ORGANIZATION means building consensus and cooperation among the groups that play roles in downtown. It also involves creating a network that is well represented by those who have an important stake in downtown's economic viability. A strong volunteer-driven program and an organizational structure made up of a board of directors and committees based on the four points of Main Street™ provide the stability to build and maintain a long-term effort.

PROMOTION creates excitement downtown. Marketing the district's unique and enticing characteristics to shoppers, new businesses, and visitors can be an effective promotional strategy to build a positive image. Well-thought-out marketing campaigns include advertising, retail promotional activities, and special events.

DESIGN enhances the attractiveness of the business district and creates an inviting atmosphere. Historic building rehabilitation, quality window displays, colorful banners, well-maintained sidewalks, landscaping, and street lighting all improve the physical image of downtown and help make it a desirable place to shop, work, walk, invest, and live. Design conveys a visual message about the downtown and what it has to offer.

ECONOMIC RESTRUCTURING strengthens the economic base of a downtown area while diversifying it. Economic restructuring activities include helping existing downtown businesses expand, recruiting new businesses to provide a balanced mix, converting unused space into productive property, and sharpening the competitiveness of business enterprises.

Communities may undertake downtown revitalization activities using the National Main Street Approach™. However, in order to become a National Main Street Program, the community must assure that the following criteria is in place:

- ▸ *Broad-based community support from the public and private sectors*
- ▸ *Vision and mission statements relevant to community conditions and to the local Main Street Program's organizational stage*
- ▸ *Comprehensive Main Street work plan*
- ▸ *Historic preservation ethic*
- ▸ *Active board of directors and committees*
- ▸ *Adequate operating budget*
- ▸ *Paid professional program manger*
- ▸ *Program of ongoing training for staff and volunteers*
- ▸ *Reporting of key statistics*
- ▸ *Current member of the National Main Street Network*

✿ SNAPSHOTS ✿

Main Street Programs have experienced $35.10 in new investment for every $1 spent to administer the program.

Main Street Programs have shown a net gain of 174,000 new jobs and 47,000 new businesses.

Just the Basics

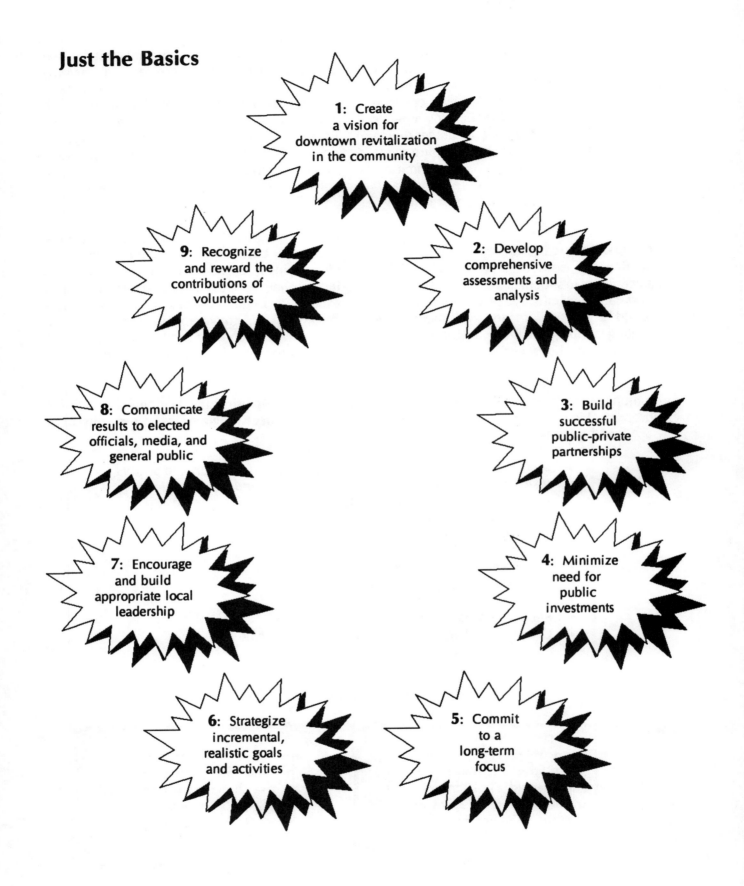

1: Create a vision for downtown revitalization in the community

2: Develop comprehensive assessments and analysis

3: Build successful public-private partnerships

4: Minimize need for public investments

5: Commit to a long-term focus

6: Strategize incremental, realistic goals and activities

7: Encourage and build appropriate local leadership

8: Communicate results to elected officials, media, and general public

9: Recognize and reward the contributions of volunteers

DOWNTOWN REVITALIZATION PLAN

Activity	Description	Champion	Budget	Start Date	End Date
Concept	The concept of central business district improvements and their importance is sold to the community.				
	Measurement: The community is talking about the importance of revitalizing the central business district.				
Organizational Development	Form an organizational committee to establish a main street/central business district improvement program.				
	Measurement: The organizational committee is meeting regularly.				
Downtown Assessment	Inventory downtown area for number of buildings, usage, size, amenities, services, traffic routes, infrastructure, problems, and potential usage.				
	Measurement: Inventory list and map of downtown area are now available.				
Research Historic Features	Identify unique character of any building or area and any historic events that took place at the site(s).				
	Measurement: Historic landmarks are documented.				
Plan Development	The committee develops its plans through internal assessment, reviewing other projects, and professional assistance, if necessary.				
	Measurement: Plan is drafted and completed.				
Committees	Organize key committees for promotion, design, and economic restructuring.				
	Measurement: Committees established and functioning.				
Funding	Secure funds for specific projects identified in the plan.				
	Measurement: The money is in the bank.				
Implementation	Undertake projects selected as a result of this planning effort.				
	Measurement: The plan is implemented.				

Downtown Revitalization at a Glance

What can you expect to accomplish?

- ❏ Establishment of a future vision for the downtown area
- ❏ Increased customer patronage with downtown businesses
- ❏ Increased customer traffic within the downtown

- ❏ Increased property values and tax revenue generated within the downtown
- ❏ Dramatic visual and aesthetic improvements
- ❏ Extensive press coverage

Who will do the work?

- ❏ Local government or committee thereof
- ❏ Chamber of Commerce or committee thereof

- ❏ Separately established body with or without designated staff
- ❏ Volunteers

How will you pay for these activities?

- ❏ City government general fund or special dedicated funds
- ❏ Corporate donations
- ❏ Federal or state grants

- ❏ Fund-raising events/ product sales
- ❏ Sponsorships/retail fees
- ❏ Memberships
- ❏ Historic preservation tax credits

What role does the board member play?

- ❏ Sponsorship of committee or oversight group
- ❏ Actively participates on committee or organization
- ❏ Educates and builds consensus for downtown activities

- ❏ Fund-raising
- ❏ Helps maximize volunteer activity
- ❏ Ensures that projects and activities are consistent with downtown goals and objectives

What Success Looks Like

It had been four years since Ed first met Andrea for lunch. During that time, they had lots of meals and meetings together, as they had been part of a task force to address downtown redevelopment. Now they were meeting for lunch again—this time to celebrate.

The task force had completed a comprehensive inventory of downtown businesses and buildings. After receiving some local and state grants to help fix up the downtown area, they began recruiting small businesses and entrepreneurs. The task force had also developed a wish list of businesses they would like to see in the area. One of the first companies to set up shop was a music store specializing in fiddles, offering sales, repair, and instruction. To boost sales, the store owners decided to sponsor a fiddle contest. In the first year, sales had increased so much that they were able to purchase street lamps in the design of a fiddle. The following summer, the town sponsored a very successful fiddle festival.

Several businesses relocated after attending the festival. The downtown area slowly began to come alive as more and more people discovered Field. Now, there wasn't a single available building *not* being put to some productive use.

As Ed walked to the new restaurant, he saw the headlines of the local paper announcing the third annual *Fiddle Around in Field Festival.* Contestants were there from all over the country, and every hotel room was booked. He noticed that the town was full of shoppers and sightseers, the sidewalks bustling with activity. A sense of vibrancy was in the air. And the fiddle festival was now on the state's must-see list in the tourism catalogue. Ed was even negotiating with some entrepreneurs who wanted to put a fiddle museum in the downtown area.

When Ed met Andrea at the restaurant, the hostess asked if they had a reservation. Ed and Andrea looked at each other, somewhat shocked. "No," he replied. "How long a wait will it be?"

"About thirty minutes," she responded.

Ed was hungry, but he was more than happy to wait and watch people enjoy themselves with all their downtown purchases by their side.

REFERENCES

Lawhead, Terry. "A Comprehensive Strategy for Rural Downtowns," *Economic Development Review*, Volume 13, Number 2, Spring 1995.

Miller, David. *Niche Strategies for Downtown Revitalization.* Downtown Research and Development Center.

Revitalizing Downtown. National Trust for Historic Preservation, American Planning Association.

RESOURCES: The National Main Street Center can be reached at:

National Main Street Center
National Trust for Historic Preservation
1785 Massachusetts Avenue NW
Washington DC 20036
Phone 202-588-6219

Chapter 6: **BUSINESS PARKS**

While Ed was doing his economic development research, he received a call from Sally, the president of the Chamber of Commerce in a nearby community. Sally had lived in the East most of her life, but moved to the Northwest to enjoy the wide-open spaces and get away from the crime and pollution.

"Ed," she said, "I'd like you to join me in meeting a prospect who wants to develop an aerospace guidance control manufacturing facility. You know, my town has just completed a business park, and we're hoping this will be our first tenant. Since you're a native of the area, I know you can describe some of the amenities and regional history better than I can."

Ed was thrilled for several reasons. The planning group in Field had been considering a business park of their own, so here was his chance to see one and learn about them. He hadn't participated in a site visit before and knew he could learn a lot from Sally, a former site consultant for a big firm in New Jersey. Plus, he loved to share stories about the area's rich history and how wonderful the area was for recreation and raising children.

Sally and Ed met the prospect when his plane landed at the regional airport equidistant between Ed and Sally's towns. Since the prospect was her lead, Sally fielded most of the questions. As she drove towards her town and pointed out landmarks, Ed added some historical perspective and personal anecdotes about many of them.

When Sally reached the downtown area, she drove especially slow so the prospect could see the variety of stores and bustling activity. She pointed to new signage and streetlights and the cobblestone sidewalks. "This street is closed to traffic on Saturdays in summer for a farmers market during the day and a music festival featuring local artists at night. It's really livened up the town."

Sally then drove through residential areas and explained how the town was laid out. The schools and shopping areas had been located with the residential areas in mind, and parks were an integral part of the entire community. She told the prospect how concentrating like-land uses made great sense in the Northwest. Where she had come from, houses were located next to factories and landfills were near downtowns. Ed could see the prospect taking notes and making diagrams.

Resources Clipboard

High
Med
Low

People   Time   Money

Sally then took the prospect to the business park on the outskirts of town. The prospect pulled out a camera and began shooting. "This area is construction-ready and zoned to allow companies with similar activities and needs to locate together," Sally explained. "It also allows for efficiency as to economy of scale. We put in well-paved roads to support truck traffic, and the water mains were sized to accommodate the high-pressure needs of industry." She mentioned the power company could deliver electricity at the wattage and phasing necessary for industrial use, and telecommunications cables were also installed. Ed saw that the prospect was really impressed.

They walked around the property for almost two hours. The prospect asked all sorts of questions about covenants, permitting, and wetlands. Sally had answers for all of his questions. As they walked back to the car, Sally showed him a document from the State Department of Ecology indicating that the property was pre-permitted for development within certain parameters. The client asked if he could have a copy, and Sally provided him one on the spot. Later that afternoon, on the drive back to the airport, the prospect said, "I'll be back in touch with you, Sally. This site is definitely one of my top three."

The visit convinced Ed that he still had a lot of work to do before his town was ready for a business park—let alone a prospect. Ed had believed that because his community was surrounded by accessible agricultural land, they had ample space available for a business park. But he learned from Sally that having undeveloped land did not mean a business park would automatically appear.

What is a Business Park?

A business park is an area of land set aside for commercial and industrial purposes. No residential buildings are allowed within the park, and the site is typically established away from residential areas to lessen the impact of noise, traffic, and other aspects of industry. The park must be consistent with a master plan and zoning restrictions to achieve the following objectives:

* ★ Consistency with community goals.
* ★ Efficient business and industrial operations.
* ★ Compatibility with natural environments.
* ★ Sustaining highest land values.

Why is Business Park Development Important?

In the competitive world of economic development, success is directly related to the preparation and creation of necessary tools to close deals. A successful business park development plan is one of the most important tools. The plan will help you:

* ▶ Focus your economic development effort.
* ▶ Infuse the community with capital investment.
* ▶ Link similar developments in a defined location.
* ▶ Minimize infrastructure investment.
* ▶ Provide a variety of employment opportunities.
* ▶ Create substantial property tax revenue.
* ▶ Generate secondary support businesses.
* ▶ Strengthen local businesses that act as suppliers.
* ▶ Minimize negative impacts of development.
* ▶ Keep truck traffic away from residential areas.

CHARACTERISTICS OF
BUSINESS PARK DEVELOPMENT

GROUP EFFORT

It takes many players, acting in partnership, to make a development project successful.

LONG-TERM PROCESS

It takes a number of steps to develop a business park. This will not occur overnight.

NEEDS SUBSTANTIAL UP-FRONT CAPITAL

The more you can develop your business park before the prospect arrives, the better your chances of closing the sale. Financing can be through traditional methods or creative partnerships.

REQUIRES LEADERSHIP AND VISION

Constructing a business park is often a leading activity for a community's economic development organization. You must be willing to take a leadership position.

Developing a Business Park

Business parks are not a new idea. The first park was constructed in Manchester, England, in 1896.

The five critical components to developing a business park are **market analysis, engineering analysis, planning analysis, financial analysis,** and the **implementation plan.** Your economic development organization will need to ask the following key questions about each component:

MARKET ANALYSIS

Local Construction Trends

- How much and what type of construction is occurring in your community?
- What new business construction projects are taking place?
- How many acres of land are utilized in development projects every year?
- Is the investment in development coming from local companies or from outside the area?
- How many jobs are created?

Expansion Needs

- How many companies expand each year?
- What size and type are these companies?
- Is there a timing issue associated with the expansions?
- Are there site limitations to the expansions?
- How many jobs are created?

Prospect Trends

· How many contacts or inquiries do you receive each year?
· What does the prospect look like (industry type, etc.)?
· How many jobs could they potentially create?

Lost Opportunities

· How many opportunities are lost each year due to the lack of a business park?
· How many potential jobs are lost?
· What is the real reason for the loss?

Competition

· What other industrial parks are in the area?
· What vacant buildings are around?
· What are the strengths of the competition?
· What are the weaknesses of the proposed park?

Potential for Induced Markets

· What unmet needs exist in the local market?
· What compatible uses are in the area?
· What are the historical trends for similar investment?

Area Analysis

· What is the public attitude toward this type of development?

IDEAS BANK:

■ *Demand for property can be determined by talking with local business owners. To estimate the demand, take the number of new businesses that have located or expanded in the past five years in the surrounding 25 miles. The total acreage they used can be divided by the number of years (5). Take a reasonable percentage of this figure to acknowledge the amount of market share you'll capture.*

■ *Land can be secured through zero-cost options. The key here is to get everything in writing up front.*

ENGINEERING ANALYSIS

Environmental Aspects

· What wetlands and watercourses impact the site?
· What is the hydrogeology of the site?
· Is this area protected or restricted from development?

Physical Features

· What is the topography of the site?
· Will the soils on the site support development?
· Is there sufficient drainage for this site?
· Are there any vegetation concerns?

Opportunities and Constraints

· What are the adjacent land uses?
· Are there any natural or man-made constraints?
· Are there any existing or potential site enhancements?
· What is the overall building potential for the site?

Zoning

· What is the current zoning for the site?
· What is the potential or needed zoning for the site?

TYPICAL LAND USE ACTIVITY IN INDUSTRIAL PARKS:

Light Industrial	30.5%
Office/Administration	20.1
Distribution/Warehouse	17.9
Office/Warehouse	13.1
Heavy Industrial	7.5
Research & Development/ Pilot Manufacturing	5.4
Other	5.5

IDEAS BANK:

■ Key contacts for engineering data include: regional planning commission, county planner, and county engineer.

■ Be very sensitive to environmental issues. You cannot destroy a wetland to create an industrial park.

■ Failure at this stage usually occurs when soil conditions are ignored. Remember, it takes greater soil strength to hold up a building than a field of wheat.

■ 100-year flood plains have stopped development on a number of projects. Check these maps early!

PLANNING ANALYSIS

Land Uses

· What alternative land uses should be considered?
· How can we treat any special features about this site?
· How can we optimize any attractive, natural features?

Roads

· What are the major access roads supporting this site?
· What secondary roads support this site?
· How will traffic circulate if we complete this development?
· Where should the park entrance be located?

Utilities

· What is the availability of utilities to serve this site?
· Where are the utilities located and how will they have to be rerouted?
· What are their existing sizes and capacities to facilitate new development in the community?

IDEAS BANK:

■ *A planning analysis will pick the "highest and best use" of a site. This decision will be made based upon prior developments in the area. If the community has not had a business park in the past, this will not be the recommended use. It takes true leadership at this point to make a business park a reality.*

FINANCIAL ANALYSIS

Land Acquisition

· What will this land cost to purchase?
· Who will do the appraisals and at what cost?
· What will be the legal and closing costs for this acquisition?
· How much will title insurance cost?
· Who will finance the acquisition and at what rate and term?

Infrastructure Costs

· What will the be cost of our on-site infrastructure improvements?
· What will be the cost of our off-site infrastructure?
· How are we going to handle price escalations during the various phases?

Planning and Design Costs

· How much will the engineer, land use planner and landscape designer charge for this project?

Soft Costs

· What are the unexpected start-up costs?
· What are the unexpected ongoing costs?
· How much will project administration cost?
· How much is marketing and promotion going to cost?
· What will the insurance for the project be?
· What other interest and funding costs are necessary for this project?
· What selling commissions will we incur?
· How much will the attorneys charge?
· How much will the accountants need for their services?
· What are the property management expenses?

IMPLEMENTATION PLAN

Project Design

· What is the park's design philosophy?
· What zoning restrictions apply to this park?
· What are the performance standards expected for tenants in the park?
· What will the protective covenants provide in this park?

Marketing Strategy

· What existing marketing efforts are underway?
· At what level will we staff the marketing effort?
· What printed materials will be needed for this park?
· How big will the marketing budget be?
· What marketing strategies will we utilize?

a) Relationships with brokers
b) Use of economic development agencies
c) Space advertising
d) Direct mail

e) Personal contacts
f) Initial vs. long-term efforts
g) Internet/Web site

BUSINESS PARK DEVELOPMENT PLAN

Activity	Description	Champion	Budget	Start Date	End Date
Concept	A broad discussion of the business park needs to occur.				
	Measurement: The community is talking about the importance of the park.				
Feasibility Market Analysis	Do we have sufficient market demand to warrant a business park?				
	Measurement: A figure has been developed that quantifies how fast land will be developed in the new park.				
Feasibility Engineering Analysis	Does our preferred site have the capacity to support development?				
	Measurement: Engineering analysis has been completed.				
Feasibility Planning Analysis	Are the essential community elements in place to support this project?				
	Measurement: Planning analysis has been completed.				
Feasibility Financial Analysis	Can we arrange funding to develop the business park?				
	Measurement: Financial analysis has been completed.				
Feasibility Implementation Plan	How are we going to sell this new park to the marketplace?				
	Measurement: Implementation plan was completed.				
Contract Negotiation	Formal discussions with various partners and consultants who will make this park a reality.				
	Measurement: All hired help is at the table and discussing the development plan.				
Formal Commitments	Formalize partnerships in writing.				
	Measurement: Completed contracts are in place.				
Park Development	Actual construction of the park.				
	Measurement: Dirt is being moved.				
Completion and Opening	Dedication ceremony by mayor and key officials.				
	Measurement: Local media has announced the new park.				
Marketing and Property Management	Ongoing park management throughout the sales and construction process.				
	Measurement: The marketing program is underway.				

Just the Basics

The eight key steps to real estate development, when applied to the business park, look like this:

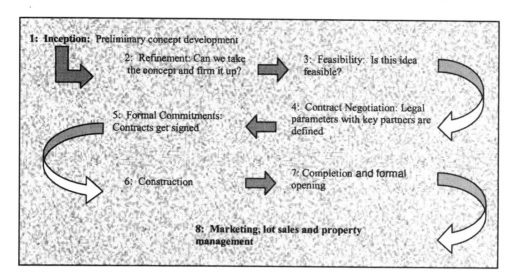

1: **Inception:** Preliminary concept development

2: **Refinement:** Can we take the concept and firm it up?

3: **Feasibility:** Is this idea feasible?

4: **Contract Negotiation:** Legal parameters with key partners are defined

5: **Formal Commitments:** Contracts get signed

6: **Construction**

7: **Completion and formal opening**

8: **Marketing:** lot sales and property management

Business Park Development a Glance

What can you expect to accomplish?

- ❑ Acreage dedicated to business expansion
- ❑ Rallying point for economic development program
- ❑ Focal point for new growth in the community
- ❑ Positive press and resulting community attitudes

Who will do the work?

- ❑ Project champions as identified in the work plan
- ❑ Contract personnel who join the project
- ❑ Governmental inspectors approving the work
- ❑ Economic development personnel

How will you pay for these activities?

- ❑ Economic development program funds
- ❑ Dedicated funds from non-general funding sources
- ❑ For-profit industrial development group or real estate investment trust (REIT)
- ❑ General fund dollars from local unit of government

What role does the board member play?

- ☐ Project oversight and guidance
- ☐ Assisting with securing partners and contractors
- ☐ Promoting lot sales from finished product
- ☐ Fund-raising for critical components, if necessary

What Success Looks Like

Ed had learned a lot from his meeting with Sally. He now knew that a business park would be a vital component of Field's economic development program.

In order to keep his community focused, he defined success by the number of steps they needed to take along the way to create a business park. In a year, he was happy to report that his community:

✓ *secured the land (1st success)*
✓ *raised the necessary funds (2nd)*
✓ *installed the infrastructure (3rd)*
✓ *executed the marketing program (4th)*
✓ *landed the first tenant (5th)*

Each step, when completed, created credibility and momentum for the local economic development effort. Ed liked that.

About a year after they first met, Ed invited Sally over to Field to see what he had accomplished. She was impressed with the appearance and completeness of his work. "If I was still in the consulting business, your park would be one I'd be happy to show to prospects," remarked Sally. "Way to go, Ed!"

∞

REFERENCES

Beyard, Mike. *Business and Industrial Park Development Handbook.* Urban Land Institute, 1995.

Business and Industrial Park Development Handbook. Community Builders Handbook Series, Urban Land Institute, 1988.

Clark, Cal. *101 Ideas on Economic Development.* People's Gas, Seattle, Washington, 1994.

Forman, Maury, and James Mooney. *The Race to Recruit.* Kendall/Hunt Publishing, Dubuque, Iowa, 1996.

Industrial Parks: A Step by Step Guide. Midwest Research Institute, 1988.

Lovorn, John, *100 Do's and Don'ts for Economic Developers.* The Pace Group, 1989.

Miles, Mike. *Real Estate Development, Principles and Process.* Urban Land Institute, 1996.

Mixed Use Business Parks. National Association of Industrial Office Parks, 1988.

Morrison, Don. *Economic Development: A Strategic Approach for Local Governments.* International City/County Management Association, 1995.

Chapter 7: SPECULATIVE BUILDINGS

Guiding Principles:

☞ Speculative building development is an expensive, controversial, and high-risk program that needs solid community support.

☞ Successful speculative building development requires a higher level of professional skill, intensive oversight during development and construction, and an aggressive sales and marketing campaign.

☞ Having available sites and buildings gives a prospective new business the opportunity to immediately choose your community as its preferred location.

☞ The size of the speculative building, the level of interior finish, and utility service must be considered in the plans.

☞ A "shell" building, where the purchaser can make many of the final finish decisions, can be a less costly alternative construction program.

☞ Proceeds from the first speculative building project may be used to develop additional sites and buildings.

☞ A vacant speculative building may financially drain an organization's resources.

Betty, a realtor and a member of Field's economic planning group, was assigned to work with Ed in preparing a list of all available industrial and commercial buildings on the market. The planning group thought they should have property available to show a prospective company that may be interested in expanding or relocating. Many members of the group still dreamed that a company would just move right into the area.

Betty compiled a list of available property on the Multiple Listing Service, as well as sites she discovered on the Internet. Several were small downtown stores under 5,000 square feet, and a couple had been vacant for more than two years. One old two-story brick building was currently being used for storage by the owner, but it needed a new roof. There was a 10,000-square-foot metal building just outside of town formerly used as a machine shop, but it had no municipal utilities. The last building on the list was a large concrete building abandoned several years ago when a locally-owned business ceased operations due to suspected environmental problems.

Ed felt a little disappointed. Obviously, none of the buildings had tempted local companies to expand, and Ed knew they wouldn't entice a company to relocate to Field, either. He also knew that once a company made a decision involving a new building, it wanted to act quickly. All of the available property needed too much work, meaning too much time before a company could start operations. The alternative would be for the community to speculate on a building for potential tenants, then build it.

With Betty's help, Ed interviewed all the real estate developers in the community and surrounding cities. They found out that developers wanted a guarantee: If they were going to build a building, a company would need to buy it within a reasonable time.

But Ed knew there were no guarantees in economic development. If the community wanted a new or expanding company in their town, they could increase their chances for success by constructing a building on speculation. Ed felt that this was the right strategy for Field,

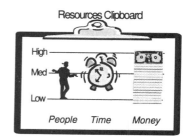

Resources Clipboard

and if local developers wouldn't take the lead in constructing a building, then the economic development group would have to find someone who would.

The planning group, Ed believed, needed to understand that this strategy would complement their vision of business expansion and job creation. But they would be taking a major risk. Being ready too soon could result in an empty building for a long time. Being ready too late may mean losing a prospective client to another community that had a building ready for occupancy. The group would need to carefully weigh the pros and cons.

What is Speculative Building Development?

Speculative building development is a defined program to acquire land, prepare plans for development of the site, install site infrastructure, and construct a commercial or industrial building for the purpose of offering it to a prospective business.

An economic development organization constructs a building with the goal of recouping all invested funds at some point in the future. The speculative building development program is intended to provide sites and buildings for a new or expanding business when the private sector does not fulfill this need.

A speculative building can be a fully constructed, ready-to-utilize building, or a shell building where contractors are hired to finish electrical and mechanical systems and pour the floor to meet the needs of the incoming business. In many cases, a shell building is more competitive due to its higher flexibility and lower construction costs. Development costs for a "spec building" typically range between $2.50 and $5.00 per square foot.

Why is Speculative Building Development Important?

Creates a Market	Speculative building development may be the only way to entice a business to locate in your community.
Development Suited to Target Industry	A community can design a speculative building to attract specific types of companies or manufacturers.
Can Be Done in Phases	A shell building may be more marketable than a completed structure, and it allows the community to complete the project in defined steps.
Can Be a Continuing Program	Upon sale of an initial building, proceeds can be used for a second project, thus establishing a revolving building program.
Potential for Long-term Income	In lieu of a sale, many businesses may want a long-term lease, which will provide ongoing income to the owner or organization. Many ports prefer this method.

CHARACTERISTICS OF SPECULATIVE BUILDINGS

HIGHLY CONTROVERSIAL

Gaining community support is more difficult than other programs because of costs, uncertainty of whether the building will sell, and the pretense of doing private sector development.

LONG TERM

From start to finish, a speculative building may require up to a year for planning, securing funding, and construction.

VERY HIGH RISK

Actively marketing a speculative building is no assurance it will be occupied in a short time period.

EXPENSIVE

Land purchase, site development, and building construction could easily require $200,000 to $1,000,000 before the building can be offered for occupancy.

REQUIRES CREATIVE FINANCING

Economic development organizations rarely have large amounts of cash or collateral to construct a building and therefore must find funding sources.

Just the Basics

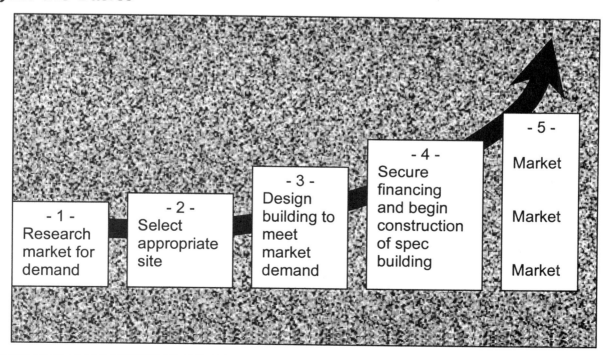

- 1 -
Research market for demand

- 2 -
Select appropriate site

- 3 -
Design building to meet market demand

- 4 -
Secure financing and begin construction of spec building

- 5 -
Market

Market

Market

QUESTIONS TO ASK

- ◆ *Is the market strong enough to consider constructing a spec building?*
- ◆ *Is there a need for more space?*
- ◆ *What are the vacancy rates for existing buildings?*
- ◆ *What is the market activity level?*
- ◆ *What are the absorption rates?*
- ◆ *What construction is currently under way?*
- ◆ *Where is a good location to build?*
- ◆ *Is the cost of this project in line with other buildings already on the market?*

(SOURCE: *Office and Industrial Properties*, June 1998.)

SPEC BUILDING DEVELOPMENT PLAN

Activity	Description	Champion	Budget	Start Date	End Date
Concept	Favorable public opinion is sought for the spec building.				
	Measurement: The community is talking about the importance of the building and its value in stimulating new investment.				
Location and Size	Wise selection of a location for the building and determination of the appropriate size.				
	Measurement: Building committee consensus about the location of the building has been achieved.				
Engineering and Design	The needs of and ideas about the building reduced to architectural drawings and specifications.				
	Measurement: Blueprints are available for review.				
Funding	Capital necessary to complete the project.				
	Measurement: Funding secured.				
Construction	Actual building of the building.				
	Measurement: A building exists.				
Completion and Opening	Dedication ceremony by mayor and key officials.				
	Measurement: Local media has announced the new building.				
Marketing and Sale	Ongoing marketing of the property for ultimate sale or lease.				
	Measurement: New company sets up in town.				

Speculative Building Development at a Glance

What can you expect to accomplish?

- [ ] Construction of a building to attract a new business

- [ ] More prospective businesses looking over your community as a place to locate

- [ ] Increased jobs and investment in the community

- [ ] Regional and statewide notoriety as a place to establish a new business

- [ ] Revitalized interest in the commercial and industrial real estate market

Who will do the work?

- [ ] An oversight committee of the economic development organization

- [ ] Other economic or community development agency in partnership

- [ ] Outside partner, private developer, utility company, port authority, community development company, etc.

How will you pay for these activities?

- [ ] Local government funds

- [ ] Private donations, dues, or other funds

- [ ] State and/or federal grants and loans

- [ ] Private or utility developer

- [ ] Ports

- [ ] Public development authorities

What role does the board member play?

- [ ] Sponsorship and oversight

- [ ] Fund-raising

- [ ] Partners in joint partnership

What Success Looks Like

Betty and Ed were pleased with the speculative building development effort. Within two years their economic development organization was able to raise more than $100,000 in donations and grants to buy five acres of land and construct a 20,000-square-foot building.

Ed saw that his recommended speculative building program was starting to pay off. Several prospective businesses visited Field and toured the building. While this was encouraging, Ed realized that a business occupying the building would be the ultimate measure of success.

∞

REFERENCES

Beyard, Michael. *Business and Industrial Park Development Handbook*. Urban Land Institute, Washington, DC.

Council for Urban Economic Development. *The Planning and Development of an Industrial Park*. Available from the American Planning Association.

Devine, James. "Creating a Simple Spec Building Program: The Example of Glendale, Arizona." *Practicing Economic Development*, 3rd edition, American Economic Development Council Educational Foundation, 1996.

SECTION III.

MARKET
DEVELOPMENT

Chapter 8:

NEW RESIDENT ATTRACTION

**While Ed was on his way to meet Bart for lunch, he tried to think of how he could convince him to make a presentation at the economic development planning group meeting next week.** Ed had met Bart on the river while he was fishing one day. Bart had paddled his kayak over to Ed and asked how the trout were biting. They struck up a friendship over the following weeks as the two continued to cross paths.

Bart had moved to Field after visiting while he was on vacation several years before. He liked the area and the town, but the major draw was the whitewater rapids. Bart loved whitewater kayaking and was on the river several times a week.

Ed soon discovered that Bart had his own business with sales of close to a million dollars last year. Bart designed "info-tainment" software, mostly used in schools, to teach kids while entertaining them at the same time with very interactive graphics. Bart had demonstrated his product to Ed on several occasions, and Ed had been very impressed. This cutting-edge technology would be the future of learning in schools, Bart predicted. Ed's children were more familiar with the product than Ed and enjoyed using it in school and at home.

Bart represented a new type of business person: a "lone eagle." He worked alone and used computers and modems so was not location-dependent. Bart enjoyed living in a rural community where the lifestyle was less competitive than the big city. He hoped to raise children in the town of Field, where people were friendly and the environment was pretty and safe.

The economic development planning group was always looking for ways to attract new money to town, and Ed had presented several options to them. They could devise a program to attract retired couples, or working couples who wanted to get out of the rat race of the city and focus on raising their families

(cocooning, it was called), or couples who were transitioning into a slower paced life, but not totally retired yet. One of the more intriguing options was the Lone Eagle Program.

At first Ed had discounted it because he couldn't imagine why independent wealthy people would consider moving to Field. But after meeting Bart, he felt that his town could offer lone eagles just as much as the next town. Before Ed started doing economic development work, the only Lone Eagle he had heard of was Charles Lindberg. What would it take to get more people like Bart to move to the community?

Ed didn't know if Bart would be willing to talk about his business to the group or not, but he might at least share some information about why he had moved his business to their town. This could lead to some very interesting recruitment possibilities....

What is New Resident Attraction?

New resident attraction, sometimes called migrant attraction, targets specific individuals or groups with disposable income to support commercial activity in the community. Making an area attractive to people interested in relocating to an area involves developing the amenities they find desirable and possibly providing some incentives to encourage their move.

People who move from one area to another are often looking for pleasant, comfortable places compatible with their lifestyles. They typically have steady incomes and are not vulnerable to normal down cycles in the national economy. Their income is often used for discretionary spending, which usually occurs locally and leads to economic development and job creation for the community.

Why is New Resident Attraction Important?

Increases Retail Sales	Migrants either bring money with them or earn a great deal and tend to spend it locally.
Creates a Multiplier Effect	Dollars spent on goods and services are re-circulated several times through the local economy.
Increases the Number of Local Jobs	Jobs follow people with money the same way that industrial payrolls generate jobs.
Helps Retain Jobs	Most targeted groups, such as retirees or loan eagles, do not compete with other residents for local jobs.
Improves Local Tax Base	Spending by new residents increases tax revenues from retail sales and property tax payments.
Increases Local Capital Pool	Money in local banks provides additional loan capital to residents.
Larger Pool of Volunteers	New residents may want to be involved in the community and bring fresh ideas and new experiences.

AREAS OF CONCERN

Despite the low cost and appealing qualities that may come with new resident attraction, communities must recognize the realities of such a strategy before they focus their time and energy in developing a marketing plan:

   ⊗ *Some communities do not have the amenities to attract people with disposable incomes.*

   ⊗ *Migrant attraction may not improve existing local industrial and agricultural enterprises, which oftentimes have been the mainstay of communities for several generations.*

   ⊗ *Communities may see increases in low-paying jobs and high-paying salaries, but not in middle-income positions, which may create resentment or hostility among residents.*

   ⊗ *It may take several years to realize substantial economic benefits from a new resident development program.*

   ⊗ *Many people who reside in small, rural communities do so because few people live there. Newcomers may not be welcomed by everybody in town.*

✿ SNAPSHOTS ✿

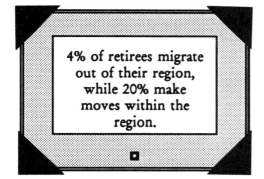

4% of retirees migrate out of their region, while 20% make moves within the region.

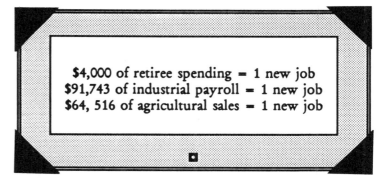

$4,000 of retiree spending = 1 new job
$91,743 of industrial payroll = 1 new job
$64, 516 of agricultural sales = 1 new job

ASSESSING THE POTENTIAL TO ATTRACT MIGRANTS

Community assessment is a major step in developing a new resident attraction campaign. Here are basic questions to answer:

1. What amenities does my community offer to people with disposable income?
2. What resources are available to serve them?
3. How many new residents can my community absorb?
4. At what rate can we absorb them into the community?
5. Are current residents receptive to welcoming new people as citizens and not just as tourists?
6. What competition do we face from other communities?
7. What changes will have to be made to accommodate new people?
8. What problems should we anticipate?
9. What types of people would be interested in moving to our community?

CHARACTERISTICS OF A NEW RESIDENT ATTRACTION PROGRAM

MULTI-YEAR STRATEGY

*Results from this effort will not occur overnight.
Your organization must be willing to build this program
over several years.*

LOW RISK

*The amount of up-front money is modest, so
the risk of failure is fairly low.*

HIGH PROFILE

*Recruiting urban dwellers to a rural
community will generate a great deal of
press and discussion in the community.*

REQUIRES CREATIVE MARKETING

*Competition with other communities trying
to attract people with disposable income is
high. Your community must be promoted as
a desired place to visit and live.*

COLLABORATIVE

*Working with a tourist bureau or Welcome
Wagon people can enhance the community's
ability to attract migrants.*

PARADIGM SHIFT

*Different lifestyles or voting tendencies
may change the character of some
rural communities.*

INCREASED DEMAND FOR SERVICES

*An influx of people will place a greater
demand on the public services and
infrastructure of the community.*

TARGET MARKETS

A number of groups can be targeted for your economic development campaign. The key is to market to people who have been to your community and enjoy visiting. It is up to you to encourage them to take the next step so that they recognize your community is a place to be year round, for most of the year, or for a second home.

Three types of people are primary targets for boosting a community's economic development efforts:

Lone Eagles   *Often referred to as knowledge workers, this group includes consultants, free-lance professionals, financial advisors, writers, and others who live by their wits and prefer to be their own boss. They can live and work anywhere and often only require a computer, fax, modem, and express mail service to be linked to the outside world.*

Retirees   *Due to vastly improved pension arrangements, this growing sector is younger, healthier, wealthier, and more active than retirees of past generations. After years of living in the city, they may be ready for the rural life.*

Cocooners   *Sometimes known as homesteaders, they have packed their bags and decided to move to a more quiet and safe community. They want to raise their families away from crowded schools, high taxes, and environmental problems and are willing to reduce their standard of living in exchange for the comforts of a rural area. Sometimes they bring a storefront business with them.*

Regardless of who you target, you'll soon see how neatly the various market segments interact and how much they contribute to the local economy. A new resident attraction program shows how you can grow a local economy without investing a lot of money in incentives and infrastructure.

WHAT SOME TOWNS HAVE DONE

✿ **Rolfe, Iowa**, population 710, showed an 11% reduction between the 1980 and 1990 censuses. Businesses were closing, and people were moving out of town. To stimulate new residential development, the town leaders offered a free lot, $1,200 up-front cash, 8.8% home mortgage (very competitive at the time), and a free one-year membership pass for golf and swimming at the local country club.

✿ **Hamilton, Missouri**, a town of 1,582, found that a major source of the local economic base came from transfer payments to senior citizens. Pretty soon, local merchants began to change their inventory to meet the needs of those people. As they did, sales began to improve, which reduced the amount of leakage of capital from the local economy. Consequently, seven new downtown businesses sprung up and a private nursing home expanded, which created 40 new jobs in the community.

✿ **Steamboat Springs, Colorado**, imposed substantial restrictions against development and totally outlawed industrial development. But it does actively promote its Lone Eagle Program. Lone eagles have generated between $50,000 and $150,000 per year in sales without using tax incentives from local government. Ten of them now have gross revenues of more than $1 million.

WHO WILL YOUR COMMUNITY ATTRACT?

TYPE OF MIGRANT	Lone Eagles	Retirees	Cocooners/ Homesteaders
EXAMPLES	• Wealthy entrepreneurs • Venture capitalists	• Active Affluents (55-64, near or recently retired) • Active Retireds (65-75, people with money)	• Newcomers to rural living • Returning to roots
CHARACTER-ISTICS	• Technologically oriented • Usually wealthy • Require limited resources • Independent	• Active and mobile • Looking to retire • Good citizens	• May bring their own business with them • Family oriented
RISKS	• Spend money outside community • Pick up and move at will • Vote like urbanites	• Drain on health services • Fixed income • Prefer to rent rather than pay property taxes • Vote against school improvements	• Burden on school system • Underemployed • Different lifestyles
INDUSTRIES THAT WILL BENEFIT	• Financial • Recreational • Utilities • Housing	• Health care • Transportation • Restaurants	• Schools • Retail
AMENITIES REQUIRED	• Telecommunications • Natural attractions	• Comprehensive health care • Transit services • Mild year-round climate	• Good schools • Safe streets • Family events • Recreational activities
JOB CREATION POTENTIAL	• Low	• Low/moderate	• Low/moderate
MODEL PROGRAMS	• Steamboat Springs, Colorado	• Sequim, Washington • Hamilton, Missouri	• Rolfe, Iowa
SAMPLE INCENTIVES	• Recreational packages • Low-interest mortgage	• Country club memberships • Moving assistance	• Land acquired through a gift or estate • Retail discounts

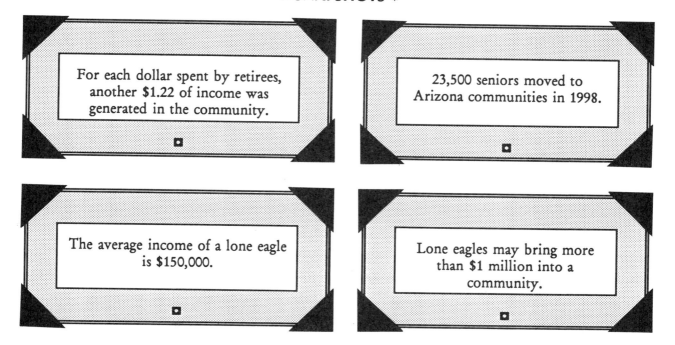

For each dollar spent by retirees, another $1.22 of income was generated in the community.

23,500 seniors moved to Arizona communities in 1998.

The average income of a lone eagle is $150,000.

Lone eagles may bring more than $1 million into a community.

Just the Basics

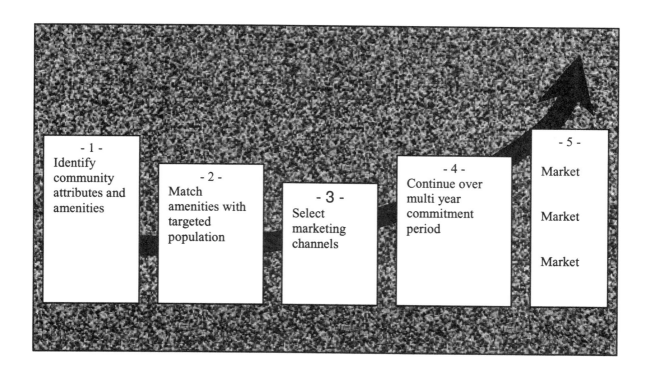

- 1 -
Identify community attributes and amenities

- 2 -
Match amenities with targeted population

- 3 -
Select marketing channels

- 4 -
Continue over multi year commitment period

- 5 -
Market

Market

Market

NEW RESIDENT ATTRACTION PLAN

Activity	Description	Champion	Budget	Start Date	End Date
Concept	The community decides that it wants to grow and that it needs to increase population before other types of investment can occur.				
	Measurement: The community is talking about the importance of and types of growth it will attract and support.				
Committee Development	A new resident attraction committee is formed to create a plan.				
	Measurement: Structure is now provided to the concept.				
Community Input Solicited	The committee conducts interviews with a number of key persons to get input regarding an attraction plan for the community.				
	Measurement: The committee has ensured that citizen input into the plan is achieved.				
Plan Development	The new resident attraction committee develops its plans and refines them to meet community goals and expectations.				
	Measurement: Marketing plan is drafted and completed.				
Public Review	Citizen hearings are conducted to allow for review of the marketing plan.				
	Measurement: Public review and comment is received.				
Plan Revision	Based on citizen comments, the marketing plan would be amended to reflect community input.				
	Measurement: The new resident attraction committee revises its plan to incorporate community opinions.				
Funding	Funding for specific projects identified in the plan needs to be secured.				
	Measurement: The money is in the bank.				
Implementation	Projects are prioritized and work gets under way.				
	Measurement: The plan is implemented.				

New Resident Attraction at a Glance

What can you expect to accomplish?

- ❏ Increased population in your community
- ❏ More sales in local businesses

- ❏ Additional jobs created to meet retail and service demand increases
- ❏ More traffic on your major roads

Who will do the work?

- ❏ Project-specific oversight committees

- ❏ Outside partners, such as realtors, religious organizations, and banks

How will you pay for these activities?

- ❏ Economic development program funds

- ❏ Special initiative fund-raising activities

What role does the board member play?

- ❏ Sponsorship and oversight
- ❏ Fund-raising

- ❏ Partners in joint partnership

What Success Looks Like

Bart gave a wonderful presentation to the planning group. In fact, he even gave free samples of his software to everyone, and they shared it with their children, grandchildren, nieces and nephews. As a result of his presentation, he received several large orders from school systems the next year.

Bart also became one of the community's best salesman. He invited some of his college friends to go kayaking with him and convinced them to move their families and their companies to the area.

The planning committee instructed Ed to work with the tourism agency at the local and state level to promote the natural and beautiful surroundings in the area. He encouraged the hotels, bed and breakfasts, and resorts to offer weekend specials and discount rates to people who completed a survey about their recreational preferences and their profession. The hospitality businesses then passed on the names and addresses to Ed, who identified potential lone eagles.

Ed contacted these people and began selling them on the amenities that Field offered year round. He received numerous positive responses, and several people decided to move to Field. The result was a substantial benefit to the entire area.

∞

REFERENCES

Beyers, William B., et al. "Lone Eagles and Other High Fliers in Rural Producer Services." Paper presented at the Pacific Northwest Regional Economic Conference, Missoula, Montana, May 1995.

Bonfante, Jordan. "Sky's the Limit," *Time*, September 6, 1993, pp. 20-27.

Fisher, Lee. *The Art of Retirement: An Economic Development Program for Rural and Distressed Areas.* January 1989.

Greising, David. "The Boonies are Booming," *Business Week*, October 9, 1995, pp. 104-109.

Lazer, William. "Inside the Mature Market," *American Demographics*, March 1995.

Severinghaus, John B. *Economic Expansion Using Retiree Income: A Workbook for Rural Washington Communities.* January 1990.

Chapter 9:

PARTNERSHIPS

Guiding Principles:

☞ It pays for communities to collaborate rather than compete.

☞ All partners must be involved from the beginning.

☞ Major players and decision makers need to be included in the process.

☞ Parties must have equal access to relevant information.

☞ Establish goals common to all participants.

☞ Create a vision whose success is based on regional cooperation.

☞ Understand the factors that influence a community's decisions and actions.

☞ Share your strengths and weaknesses.

☞ Success will not come quickly or easily.

Ed was a little nervous about the meeting he and Sally were about to chair. But she was enthusiastic and assured him it would be fine. They had spent a lot of time researching and putting together a presentation on a community partnering idea for the annual joint Cities/County meeting that included the county commissioners and representatives of all the city councils in their county.

Sally, the president of the Chamber of Commerce in a neighboring town, had been instrumental in developing a business park in her community. But despite her hard work and efforts, only two small companies had located at the site. Her town made it onto the short lists, but never quite had all the things that prospective companies needed. Sally determined that the resources lacking in her town did exist elsewhere in the county or in neighboring counties. She felt that if the area pulled together, they could offer companies a very comprehensive package.

Sally had first approached Ed about the idea of community partnering several months ago, and when he presented it to his economic development planning group, they weren't easily swayed. Ed swore those annual football rivalries did more harm than good sometimes, and it was hard to convince some of the planning group members that joining together with their traditional rivals could benefit all of them. There was a lot of discussion over "fair shares" of both expenses and benefits. In the end, however, they agreed to stay open-minded and supported presenting the idea to other communities.

As Sally and Ed made their presentation, they talked about offering employee training through the community colleges in two of the towns, working with some of the small businesses that might be interested in expanding and could provide goods and services to each other. They mentioned the possibilities of joint waste recycling facilities, of commuter buses between communities, of combined buying power, and expanding the regional airport.

They invited people at the meeting to "dream big." By the end of the meeting, Sally and Ed felt like they had made their point. Now, it was left to the various communities to think about and discuss.

Sally and Ed had agreed to give their presentation at public meetings in each of the communities. It would be an uphill road, but they knew if everyone pulled together they could overcome any odds.

Resources Clipboard

High
Med
Low

People   Time   Money

What are Partnerships?

Partnering is the process of joining with other key groups within your community or in surrounding communities to make things happen. This will allow a community to expand its market of products and services to existing and relocating businesses.

Economic development is a team activity, especially when you're trying to do it in small, rural communities where the resources to accomplish community goals are much more sparse than in urban settings. Rural communities can only succeed if they learn to associate and cooperate with their neighbors, even their competitors.

Working with others allows you to achieve a certain critical mass unattainable on your own. For example, one community may have a rail line, the other an airport. One has rolling hills for residential development; another has a talented work force just laid off due to a plant closing.

Partnering creates a vital community that businesses inside and out will see as more attractive than a single defined area. The resulting links with nearby towns and cities spawn a thriving region that promotes each of the participating community's special amenities and features. Any weaknesses of one town will be overshadowed by the strengths of its neighbors.

Why are Partnerships Important?

Creates Political Influence	Elected officials and interest groups that work together show a willingness to solve problems. It also creates stronger power base for legislative action.
Creates Support Networks	The possibility of duplication and costly competition is reduced, and resources are shared.
Encourages Cost Sharing or Circuit Riding	Communities can take advantage of group discount rates, in-kind support, and cluster marketing.
Develops Collaboration and Teamwork	People will have regional pride in what they accomplished with the help of others in their area.
Helps Build Capacity	Expands components that attract and retain businesses.
Leverages Scarce Resources	Money pooled for development goes farther than individual efforts.
Enhances Credibility of Program	The more people involved, the more plausible it looks to outsiders.

Activities Get Done	Work is spread out to numerous people rather than just a few who are already overworked.
Critical Mass is Achieved	More goals are attainable when more people are involved.
Increases Efficiencies of Service Delivery	Eliminates duplication of efforts and reduces costly or unnecessary competition.

AREAS OF CONCERN

Despite the obvious benefits that come with community cooperation and partnerships, they are often difficult to achieve. Conflicts may develop and cause a well-intentioned regional economic development program to fail. Things that hamper collaboration include:

- ⊗ *Differences in base rates.*
- ⊗ *Fear of lost identity.*
- ⊗ *Fear of red ink.*
- ⊗ *Strong egos and innuendos.*
- ⊗ *Inability to compare information.*
- ⊗ *Seeing economic development as a zero-sum game.*
- ⊗ *Failure to see similarities.*
- ⊗ *Limited vision of what they can accomplish.*
- ⊗ *Little interaction among community leaders.*
- ⊗ *Communication problems.*
- ⊗ *Inability to agree on community vision.*
- ⊗ *Larger community not believing in equality.*

RECIPE FOR DISASTER

Occasionally, board members of community economic development organizations think they are the only game in town and that no one else's input, resources, or assistance is needed. This often results in a totalitarian way of doing business by the board and a "them-versus-us" attitude by others in the community.

CHARACTERISTICS OF A
PARTNERSHIP PROGRAM

HIGHLY EFFICIENT

Working together to maximize community and regional resources is the most efficient use of time and materials in any one program.

BROAD APPLICABILITY

Partnering has been successful for:
- ♦ *Scattered free-standing towns*
- ♦ *Declining stand-alone cities*
- ♦ *Metro-regional suburban communities*

LOW RISK

Usually, capital commitments are low, which fosters lower risk to the participants.

MULTI-YEAR

Results from this effort will not occur overnight. You must be willing to build this program over a 7- to 10-year period.

Just the Basics

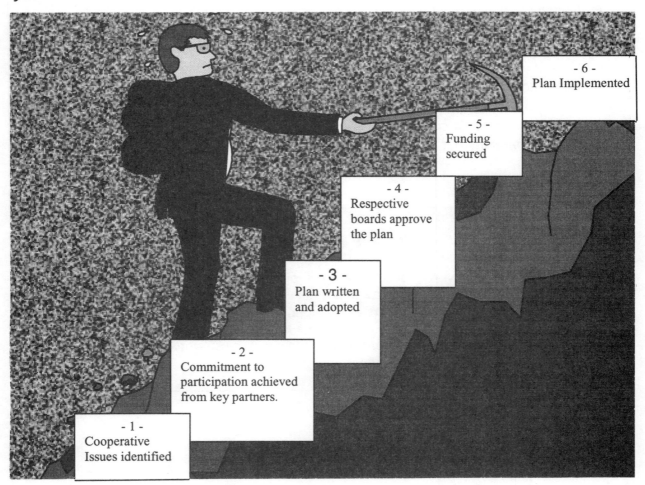

- 6 -
Plan Implemented

- 5 -
Funding secured

- 4 -
Respective boards approve the plan

- 3 -
Plan written and adopted

- 2 -
Commitment to participation achieved from key partners.

- 1 -
Cooperative Issues identified

PARTNERSHIPS WORK PLAN

Activity	Description	Champion	Budget	Start Date	End Date
Awareness	Identify those issues which cannot be solved alone.				
	Measurement: The economic development board acknowledges that it cannot solve all of the problems itself.				
Partnering	List potential partners to help address the issue.				
	Measurement: Key players in the communities are identified.				
Team Establishment	All potential members are asked to participate.				
	Measurement: Team in place and first meeting conducted.				
Plan Development	A plan of action to be adopted by the ad hoc group.				
	Measurement: Plan drafted, edited, and finalized.				
Plan Approval	Plan of action is presented to respective boards of each participant.				
	Measurement: Resolutions of support are solicited and received.				
Funding	Funding for specific projects identified in the plan needs to be secured.				
	Measurement: The money is in the bank.				
Implementation	Projects are identified as a result of this planning effort.				
	Measurement: The plan is implemented.				

Partnerships at a Glance

What can you expect to accomplish?

- ❏ Greater output from program efforts
- ❏ Increased efficiency of service delivery
- ❏ More options for economic development strategies

- ❏ More political clout
- ❏ Less stress from overwork due to outsourcing to partners
- ❏ Increase in funds to achieve goals

Who will do the work?

- ❏ Project-specific oversight committees

- ❏ Outside partners involved with each project

How will you pay for these activities?

- ❏ Economic development program funds
- ❏ Special initiative fund-raising activities

- ❏ Partners funding commitments
- ❏ Government agencies that support regional partnerships

What role does the board member play?

- ❏ Sponsorship and oversight
- ❏ Fund-raising

- ❏ Partners in joint partnership
- ❏ Credibility and leadership

What Success Looks Like

Sally and Ed were invited to dozens of small towns throughout the county to give their community partnering presentation. Though people in some communities still held grudges against others because of old football rivalries, most were in the same economic situation as the town of Field and wanted more information about how the idea would work.

Soon, people in the communities began to meet with each other to decide how they could collaborate to benefit all of the represented areas. Within a year, they developed the Network Forum, made up of service providers who lent their support to regional community and economic development activities. The group had received some money from a state program whose goal was to focus on rural communities, which assisted in:

✓ *strategic planning*
✓ *community assessment*
✓ *program evaluation*

Through efforts of the Network Forum, the communities organized retraining programs for laid-off workers, offered entrepreneurial training, and even started a micro-loan program. Businesses from all of the communities worked with the high schools, vocational schools, and community colleges to identify the skills needed to fill the jobs when companies began to grow and become competitive.

The Network Forum also helped communities establish task forces to provide input for the creation and delivery of a recruitment, retention, and leadership development program. One task force, called "Next Generation Strategies," helped lay groundwork for creating good jobs so that another generation would continue to enjoy the benefits of living in their towns.

Ed and Sally were pleased by all the things being accomplished by community cooperation.

REFERENCES

Kane, Matt, and Peggy Sand. *Economic Development: What Works at the Local Level.* American Economic Development Council.

Phillips, Phillip D., Ph.D. *Economic Development for Small Communities and Rural Areas.* University of Illinois Press.

Practicing Economic Development, 3rd edition. AEDC Educational Foundation, Rosemont, Illinois.

Wagner, Kenneth C. *Economic Development Manual.* American Economic Development Council.

Wagner, Kenneth C., Ph.D., and Maury Forman, Ph.D. *How to Create Jobs Now and Beyond 2000.* The Wagner Group, Brookline, Massachusetts.

SECTION IV.

BUSINESS DEVELOPMENT

Chapter 10: BUSINESS RETENTION AND EXPANSION

Lenny and his wife owned a well-established hotel on the edge of town. They had cultivated the habit of visiting with their guests, most of whom were business travelers and some who came to Field for recreation. The patrons enjoyed that personal touch, and it resulted in much repeat, regular business. In fact, it was one of the reasons Lenny joined the economic development planning group. He felt he could add some historical perspective about existing businesses in the community. But he was also interested in positive growth for the town. With the plant closing, fewer business guests would be coming to town, and Lenny wasn't sure how he and his wife could continue to operate.

While Lenny was on a flight home from a hotel operators' convention, he struck up a conversation with his seat mate. That gentleman was on a trip to search for a new site for his company. There simply wasn't any affordable space for him to build in the area he now was, and the local people didn't seem to care that his company was moving and taking the jobs with them. The rising property taxes and the rapid growth also made him feel as if he was being forced to move.

As he listened to the gentleman, Lenny was itching to tell him about how wonderful Field would be for his company. But he remembered the planning group retreat facilitator saying, "Look at things through other people's eyes." So Lenny asked the man about his company and what he was looking for in a new location.

They talked the whole two-hour flight. Lenny learned the man's company needed to be close to an international airport and an interstate highway, both of which left Field out of the running. Lenny also heard about what the company made, its long history, and its recent merger with several smaller companies.

He found out about the suppliers, what type of shipping they needed to have, the utility needs, and even the type of personnel required throughout the facility. Lenny was a good listener, and the man thanked him at the end of the flight for letting him go on about his company. Lenny told him it was a pleasure meeting him and wished him luck in finding a new business home.

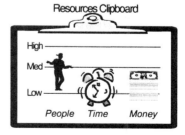

Later that evening, as Lenny drove through the streets of Field, it occurred to him that he now knew more about that stranger's business than he did about most of the businesses in his own town. Did the owners of those businesses feel like no one cared about their needs or the jobs their company provided?

Lenny decided to bring this up at the next economic development planning group meeting. He realized there was a lot of untapped potential and several opportunities already waiting for them in Field—all they had to do was find out and pay attention to what businesses and community members needed.

What is Business Retention and Expansion?

Business retention and expansion, or "BRE," as it is often called, is considered by many communities to be the cornerstone of their economic development plan. And it should be. Existing businesses provide jobs for local residents and tax revenue for the community. BRE strategy focuses on satisfying the needs of the businesses already in the community, encouraging them to stay (retains them) or grow (expand).

The most effective economic development dollars are those spent working with existing businesses, since most of the economic growth in a community is a result of established enterprises. In its simplest terms, business retention and expansion programs encourage local businesses because it shows that the community cares about them. One business location expert states he would not recommend a firm move to any community that did not have a business retention program.

A BRE strategy also builds relationships between existing employers by gathering information that will reduce business costs, improve competitiveness, increase markets, and enhance infrastructure. This information becomes the foundation of a series of programs targeted directly at the needs of the business and economic base of the community.

Why is BRE Important?

Job Growth	Expansion of a company in the same community has a more significant potential for creating jobs.
Business Stability	Companies maintain existing relationships with local suppliers and resources.
Moving is Costly	The economics of moving a company affects the company, the employees, and local community.
Stabilizes Local Tax Base	Existing companies and their employees generate revenues that pay for existing services.

Helps "At-Risk" Companies	No amount of community roots can offset poor market access or excessive costs of doing business. But removing local obstacles will increase business life span.
Provides Options	Technical assistance with bankruptcy or business succession will maintain job opportunities.
Powerful Recruitment Tool	Owners and employees of successful existing businesses are a community's best ambassadors.

CHARACTERISTICS OF BRE PROGRAMS

PROVIDE TECHNICAL ASSISTANCE
Services may include management consulting,
assisting with expansion siting, increasing competitiveness,
acting as intermediary for workforce training, or
working with local government to solve problems.

FLEXIBLE
A custom-tailored program bridges a gap
between the community's resources and the
needs of the business community.

INEXPENSIVE TO START
A small core of volunteers, organized into an
effective team of community advocates,
can start a BRE program.

COST-EFFECTIVE
Maintaining existing businesses is
significantly less expensive per job and new
investment dollar than other economic
development efforts.

EASIEST TO SERVE
It is much easier to contact a company
currently in your community through formal
or informal means than a business or
industry from outside the area.

COLLABORATIVE
Requires the cooperation of business and
local governments.

RESULTS-ORIENTED
Information is collected for the purpose of
taking positive action.

ASSISTS LONG-TERM STRATEGY
Data collected will help community focus on
long-term needs of businesses.

POLITICALLY CORRECT
Emphasis is placed on meeting the needs of
local businesses, not on wooing outsiders.

Just the Basics

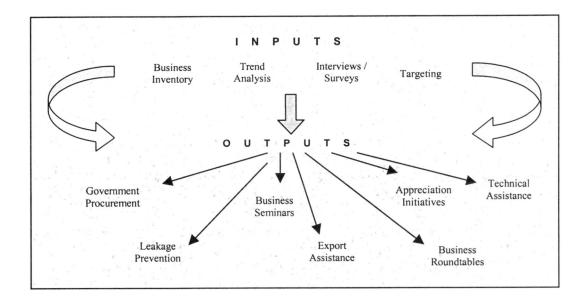

Retention and Expansion Activities

The primary focus of most expansion and retention programs is to:

▶ *Help business become more competitive in the long run.*
▶ *Remove local obstacles that could prompt existing firms to contemplate relocation of their operation.*

Before deciding on which BRE programs will achieve these results, an economic development organization should initiate a number of actions, or inputs. Most communities begin small and build upon prior experiences and successes. A continually evolving program will result in a successful effort.

INPUTS

Inputs help decision-makers understand local business and its needs. They will provide information that can lead to:

▶ *Building relationships*
▶ *Establishing long-term planning and policies*
▶ *Providing early warning signs for at-risk companies*
▶ *Identifying expansion needs*

The four main inputs are **business inventory**, **trend analysis**, **interviews** and **surveys**, and **targeting**.

BUSINESS INVENTORY

DESCRIPTION

Identify the industries from which money flows into the local economy. The primary industries are manufacturing, agriculture, export services, and tourism. The secondary industries are retail, service, construction, insurance, real estate, transportation, and communications.

TOOLS and TECHNIQUES

- Data may be collected by economic development staff or volunteers
- Information may be available in the State Treasurers' office or Employment Security office
- Tax records can provide business information

RESOURCES NEEDED

- Volunteers to collect the information
- Government reports
- State labor market reports

TREND ANALYSIS

OBJECTIVE

The BRE program must have a macro view of trends impacting the business community. For example, how effective would an expansion be in an industry currently in a recessionary phase? Having basic economic data will help the program's credibility when meeting with business community representatives.

TOOLS and TECHNIQUES

- Consult with a leading economist from either a state college or a bank in the community that is part of a regional or national chain
- Review the *Wall Street Journal*, *Forbes*, or other business newspapers and magazines

RESOURCES NEEDED

- Economic development professionals
- Resourceful people in key institutions
- Committed volunteers
- State labor market staff
- Library

INTERVIEWS/SURVEYS

OBJECTIVE

Business visitation and surveys are the core activities in a retention and expansion program, as these are how local needs and factors will be revealed.

This will lay the groundwork for determining if firms are considering relocating or closing. It will also foster public and private sector communication and build a pro-business attitude for local business by showing that they are appreciated.

TOOLS and TECHNIQUES

- Business inventory
- Target businesses at risk or those with the greatest growth potential
- Interview key people (CEOs, managers, or owners)
- Insure that interviewers have a working knowledge of business and industry
- Phone interviews are an option, but face-to-face conversations bring the greatest results
- Balance your interview team with members from both public and private sectors

RESOURCES NEEDED

- Volunteers to make contacts
- Someone to compile the data and produce reports on business community needs
- Participation from the business top management

TARGETING

In every community, time, energy, or financial resources are limited. Targeting assures the greatest impact for those expenditures. Not every company in the community needs or wants the services of a business retention program. Targeting simply directs the resources to the area of greatest need.

TARGETS

→ A geographic area. For example, an area in the community may be targeted for revitalization.
→ An industry. Research may indicate that one sector is contracting (shrinking).
→ A business sector that may be at risk (manufacturing, farm, service, retail), or a specific niche within that sector (electronic components, agribusiness, technology)
→ A group of entrepreneurs (i.e., minority, women)
→ Links to other businesses (i.e., suppliers, customers)
→ Locally-owned businesses
→ A type of worker
→ Capital expenditures budget
→ Family-owned businesses

QUICK-REFERENCE GUIDE

INPUT	Building Relationships	Planning and Policy	Early Warning	Expansion
BUSINESS INVENTORY	✔			✔
TREND ANALYSIS		✔	✔	✔
INTERVIEWS / SURVEYS	★	✔	★	★
TARGETING		★	★	★

★ *Key activity for success*
✔ *Most likely will result*

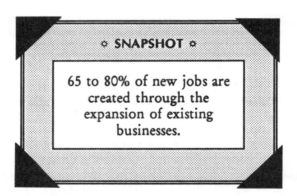

❖ **SNAPSHOT** ❖

65 to 80% of new jobs are created through the expansion of existing businesses.

Business Retention Programs

Based on the information that has been collected, an economic development organization can determine the types of assistance the business community would find helpful for increasing competitiveness and for removing local barriers. The following programs—or outputs—are examples of what other communities have developed and are not a comprehensive list.

OUTPUTS

TECHNICAL ASSISTANCE

OBJECTIVES	TECHNIQUES	RESOURCES*
• Assist in expansion efforts • Provide management consultations • Help firms solve local problems • Assist at-risk companies • Develop data to track progress • Help local leaders understand needs and conditions of economy • Provide access to capital	• Provide interviewer training program • Create inventory of locally available sites • Include public and private utilities in infrastructure decision-making and planning • Identify community and business needs from survey • Develop a referral system • Timely response and follow-up • Share nonconfidential information with local leaders for planning • Coordinate workforce needs with community colleges	• Industry journals • Informative interviewers • Knowledge of federal and state programs • Trade adjustment assistance centers • Comprehensive questionnaires • Business cooperation • Local leaders buy-in • Problem-solving government agencies that can cut red tape • Data bank of possible expansion sites • Community colleges • Public and private utilities • Revolving loan funds • Micro-loan programs

* For an excellent summary of federal and state assistance programs, see *Keeping Business Happy, Healthy and Local* by Ginger Rich, published by the Washington Department of Community, Trade and Economic Development, 1998.

BUSINESS SEMINARS

OBJECTIVES	TECHNIQUES	RESOURCES
• Develop network for employees and managers • Identify common needs • Improve ways to cut costs, improve product or service, and enhance employee morale	• Consult businesses for areas of interest • Develop programs of interest to those businesses • Bring in outside specialists • Include interactive sessions • Summarize sessions in newsletter • Have several businesses share cost of training • Offer workshops to management and employees • Have regular (not sporadic) training • Include sessions on customer service, total quality management, new technology, welfare reform, and workforce development	• Mailing lists of targeted people or businesses • Database of resources that can be brought to the community • Speakers' list • Creative curriculum • Local or statewide sponsors • Community colleges • Voc-tech schools

APPRECIATION INITIATIVES

OBJECTIVES

- Show local businesses that they are appreciated
- Provide media coverage for local businesses
- Promote economic development program

TECHNIQUES

- Solicit nominations from community
- Include public and private sector people in selecting the winners
- Recognize all nominees
- Include display of products in ceremony
- Send press release to all media
- Have local leaders make award presentation

RESOURCES

- Local sponsors
- Volunteers to help organize
- Invitations
- Media coverage
- Donations

EXPORT ASSISTANCE

OBJECTIVES

- Help diversify customer base
- Expand business operations

TECHNIQUES

- One-on-one consulting to small and medium-size companies
- Exporting assessments provided by experts in the field
- Seminars on exporting
- Awareness presentations conducted at local service organizations
- International lead generation
- Trade show assistance
- Encourage companies to become foreign trade zone subzones
- Develop list of export financing programs

RESOURCES

- Industry professionals
- Staff from the state office
- Port representative
- Trade publications
- World Trade Association
- National Trade Data Bank
- Official Export Guide
- Small Business Administration

BUSINESS ROUNDTABLES

OBJECTIVES

- Promote dialogue and strengthen relationships between government and business
- Provide a forum for business to express ideas
- Discuss issues relevant to entire community
- Provide opportunity for input in developing local policies
- Demonstrate commitment of local government to support local businesses

TECHNIQUES

- Select a neutral location to meet
- Develop issues based on community concern
- Discuss regulatory issues that impede growth
- Provide handouts that summarize issues
- Provide minutes
- Identify person to follow up on recommendations

RESOURCES

- Knowledge of business community concerns
- Information packets
- Program support
- Decision-makers buy-in
- Independent facilitator

GOVERNMENT PROCUREMENT

OBJECTIVES

- Encourage government to purchase from local vendors
- Diversify customer base
- Increase business awareness of government purchasing program

TECHNIQUES

- Understand the buying needs of governmental entities
- Coordinate seminars and direct mailings to local businesses
- Provide information of possible matches during retention interviews
- Assist in placing local companies on bidder's list
- Act as ombudsman

RESOURCES

- State procurement agencies

LEAKAGE PREVENTION

OBJECTIVES

- Decrease amount of local dollars spent outside area
- Promote local programs to purchase from local vendors
- Match local suppliers with major businesses

TECHNIQUES

- Generate reports that identify manufacturers in the state
- Make list user-friendly by segmenting it into zipcode, region, and SIC codes
- Identify other communities that have reduced leakage
- Promote vendor fairs

RESOURCES

- Supplier linkage programs
- Database of manufacturers
- List of locally produced products

BRE DEVELOPMENT PLAN

Activity	Description	Champion	Budget	Start Date	End Date
INPUT *Business Inventory*	What does the actual business inventory of this community look like? *Measurement:* A local directory of industries and businesses is completed.				
INPUT *Trend Analysis*	What business and demographic trends do I see in my community? *Measurement:* An analysis of strengths, weaknesses, and future needs is conducted.				
INPUT *Interviews/ Surveys*	What do business owners have to say about doing business here? *Measurement:* Business owners have been contacted and interviewed.				
INPUT *Targeting*	Which segments or specific companies should the BRE program assist? *Measurement:* At-risk and growth businesses have been identified.				
OUTPUT *Technical Assistance*	What are the needs of existing targeted businesses? *Measurement:* Number of businesses saved/expanded or jobs retained/created.				
OUTPUT *Business Seminars*	What technical seminars does the business community need? *Measurement:* Businesses and community colleges develop a curriculum.				
OUTPUT *Appreciation Initiatives*	How can the community show appreciation to its existing businesses? *Measurement:* Recognition events held.				
OUTPUT *Export Assistance*	How can I help businesses export their goods into foreign markets? *Measurement:* Export-ready businesses identified and assisted.				
OUTPUT *Business Roundtables*	What communication links do I need to establish in my community? *Measurement:* Monthly meetings between local leaders and business established.				
OUTPUT *Government Procurement*	How can we help businesses do business with state and local governments? *Measurement:* Businesses trained in governmental purchasing opportunities.				
OUTPUT *Leakage Prevention*	How can we keep dollars in our community? *Measurement:* Database of local producers and suppliers developed; vendor fair coordinated.				

Retention and Expansion at a Glance

What can you expect to accomplish?

- ❑ Closer working relationship with your business community
- ❑ Early warning of business concerns
- ❑ Increased local capacity to create and retain jobs

- ❑ Open lines of communication among community leadership
- ❑ Increased capacity to make things happen in your community

Who will do the work?

- ❑ Economic development staff
- ❑ Community volunteers

- ❑ Outside parties (dependencies)

How will you pay for the activities?

- ❑ Organizational dollars and in-kind donations
- ❑ Use of program sponsors
- ❑ Local government

- ❑ Support from major donors/banks
- ❑ Program operations budget

What role does the board member play?

- ❑ Program oversight
- ❑ Guidance for volunteers and economic development staff

- ❑ Direct involvement and participation with business visitations and interviews

What Success Looks Like

Three years had passed since Lenny had joined the economic development planning group. After the plant had closed, he had wondered whether he would be able to keep his hotel open. The plant had generated a lot of business for his hotel, and over the next year the room occupancy dropped considerably. He was losing a lot of money and was ready to call it quits.

Shortly after the plant closed, Ed called and asked Lenny if he would like to be interviewed by a business retention team. He didn't want to meet with them but did so as a favor to Ed. He would answer their questions, but would not discuss his thoughts of closing the hotel.

The interview was very extensive, and he was surprised at the interviewer's familiarity with hotel jargon. Not long afterwards, the BRE team met with him again and made a number of suggestions on how he could modify the way he did business. Since the hotel had been relying so much on business travelers, the team suggested that Lenny make it less of a place to stay for businessmen and more of one for families. They told him that the Visitors Business Association was planning to sponsor several family events and festivals to bring people in from out of town. So he and his wife began to reconsider: Should they really close their hotel and pack their bags, too?

Lenny didn't know if he could afford to make improvements in his hotel and pay for marketing materials. The BRE team, however, advised him of some small business loans available through a revolving loan program that the economic development group helped establish. His loan was approved and he used the money to install a hot tub and a playground.

The BRE team also sponsored management classes at the community college (which he attended) and hospitality classes for his employees. In exchange for the tuition for his employees who attended the hospitality classes, he allowed the community college to use his kitchen two mornings a week to teach a cooking and restaurant management class. Lenny later hired some of the graduates of that class.

Over the next two years, hotel occupancy greatly improved as a result of all the family activities that Field was promoting. The hotel even co-sponsored a number of events.

Now Lenny was getting dressed and ready to go to a banquet honoring his hotel as the "Turn-Around Business of the Year." He was very pleased with what he had accomplished, but he knew that if he hadn't participated in that BRE interview, he wouldn't be accepting the award tonight. He would make sure that he acknowledged all the BRE team members in his thank-you speech.

∞

REFERENCES

"A Business Retention Users Guide," *Northern Indiana: America's Industrial Resource*. Northern Indiana Public Service Company, Hammond, Indiana.

California Business Retention and Expansion Program. Office of Local Development, California Department of Commerce, Sacramento.

Hatry, Harry P., Mark Fall, Thomas O. Singer, and E. Blane Lines. *A Manual: Monitoring the Outcomes of Economic Development Programs*. The Urban Institute.

Introduction to Economic Development. Council for Urban Economic Development, Washington, DC, 1996.

Kotval, Zenia, John R. Mullin, and Kenneth Payne. *Business Attraction and Retention: Local Economic Development Efforts*. International City/County Management Association, Washington, DC, 1996.

Morse, George, editor. *The Retention and Expansion of Existing Businesses*. Iowa State University Press, Ames, 1990.

Rich, Ginger. *Keeping Business Happy, Healthy, and Local*. Washington Department of Community, Trade and Economic Development, 1998.

Winter, Eric. "Barriers to the Implementation of Economic Development Projects in Rural Texas Communities," *ED Review*, Summer 1996, vol. 14, no. 3, pp. 73-75.

Chapter 11

BUSINESS ATTRACTION

Guiding Principles:

☞ Business attraction is not—and should not—be the cornerstone of your economic development efforts.

☞ A minimum of 3 to 5 years is needed to make business attraction successful in a community.

☞ Communities need to know their competitive and comparative advantages before attempting to attract a business.

☞ More than half of business attraction prospects come from within the same state or region.

☞ Manufacturing, while not growing very much, is still a primary target sector for business attraction.

☞ Compiling day-to-day good news of your community and getting it to the prospect can be a very compelling tool.

☞ The most frequently used marketing materials are tailored responses to inquiries, general brochures, and fact sheets.

☞ Media advertising, because of its relatively high cost and questionable effectiveness, is the most controversial business prospecting tool.

Ed liked to get to the office early so that he could scan the newspapers and catch up on local and national events. He especially liked to clip stories about the positive things happening in his community or region: new businesses that opened, companies celebrating long-term anniversaries and those that were being passed down from one generation to another, and studies that indicated how wonderful the quality of life was in the region, the recreational opportunities, and the low crime rate.

Ed also liked to peruse trade journals to see what certain types of companies were doing, which ones were expanding, and where they were relocating. He studied the chosen communities to see what made them desirable.

The town of Field had come a long way since the old plant had shut down, and members of the economic development planning group were proud of their efforts. The downtown revitalization program was almost finished, and they had finally convinced the county commissioners that a business park would benefit the community, so that was under way. But not everyone understood that what they had accomplished was economic development. Quite a few had never recovered from the shutdown; they now had low-paying jobs, and their budgets were tight. When people in Field heard about a large company relocating to another area and creating hundreds of jobs, they always asked Ed when a company like that was going to look at their town.

The planning group had discussed this very issue at several meetings. Ed explained that a number of the big companies that relocated had been given rather large incentives to move. The board agreed they could not compete with those communities. Rose, the mayor, pointed out that many of those towns were regretting their hasty decisions and lack of homework. The short-term success of "winning" had been more important than the long-term consequences. It would be years before they realized any economic benefit, if they ever did.

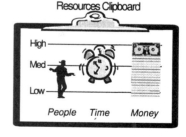

The board finally asked Ed to develop a business attraction plan. They agreed that the existing businesses were to be taken care of first, since it was much easier to keep a business than it was to recruit one. After all, it helped to have successful businesses to point to.

The planning group also knew that change in the business community was inevitable. Businesses started and either succeeded or failed. It was just part of the natural cycle of the economy. Even the best economic development efforts and a booming economy could not overcome bad management, poor customer service, or retirement and closing. The board was ready for an active effort directed toward bringing new business to the community to help offset the losses that would naturally occur.

Ed prepared a plan for presentation to his board. It would be one of the most competitive, difficult, and expensive efforts his community could undertake.

What is Business Attraction?

Business attraction focuses on identifying companies from outside the area and enticing them to expand or relocate into a community. The goal is simple and straightforward: to secure new jobs and investment. It is glamorous work, frequently commanding the most recognition of economic development efforts in local media.

The normal cycle for any business is start-up, growth, stabilization, contraction, and closure. Business attraction activities help insure that new businesses replace the ones that close.

A business attraction strategy should supplement other economic development activities and not be a community's sole focus. In fact, competition for firms is so fierce, and success so infrequent, that most authors recommend having at least three other, more viable, economic development strategies in place before tackling business attraction.

Why is Business Attraction Important?

Creates Jobs	Increases the overall health of the community.
Enhances Tax Base	Allows communities to support and improve local services without increasing taxes.
Offsets Attrition	Business closing is a normal part of economic cycle, so new businesses are needed to replace them.
Shapes Community's Future	Businesses become part of a community's long-term strategic plan.
Boosts Reputation	Communities become known for the businesses they attract.
Encourages Likely Spin-offs	Other related or competitive enterprises often follow.

CHARACTERISTICS OF BUSINESS ATTRACTION PROGRAMS

COMPETITIVE

From 15,000 to 30,000 other economic development organizations want to attract new businesses, too.

EXPENSIVE

Infrastructure investment, marketing campaigns, and incentives are required to bring a prospect to a community.

TIME-CONSUMING

Resources, personnel, and financial tools must be available for at least 3 to 5 years.

TARGET FOCUSED

Community must aim for a specific type of industry that matches community profile.

DUE DILIGENCE REQUIRED

Community must really do homework on a business to make sure that it is a sound and stable investment.

EASILY QUANTIFIABLE

Community must have specific goals when it recruits a company, such as number of jobs, capital investment, or increased tax revenues.

INCENTIVE-BASED

Almost all relocations will require some incentives. Community must conduct an economic impact analysis to assure that it is not put at risk.

FRUSTRATING

Coming in second is as frustrating as not even being considered. Business attraction has the lowest chance of success among all economic development strategies.

UNPREDICTABLE

A request for information or site visit may come at any time (often on 24 hours' notice or less). The ability to respond quickly with accurate information will increase chance of success.

QUESTIONABLE LOYALTY

Firms originating out of state are 40 times more likely to move again, compared to businesses originally established in the state.

JUST THE BASICS

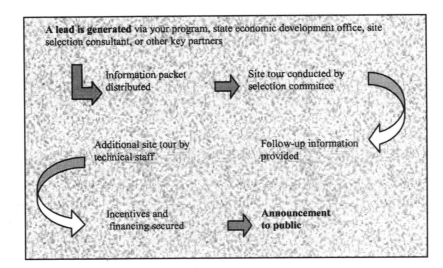

A lead is generated via your program, state economic development office, site selection consultant, or other key partners

Information packet distributed

Site tour conducted by selection committee

Additional site tour by technical staff

Follow-up information provided

Incentives and financing secured

Announcement to public

Here's how it generally works: The community, using its own self-assessment, identifies itself as a "product" and the marketable features it is selling to a business prospect. Features could be:

- *Abundance of skilled workers*
- *Low high-school dropout rate*

- *State-of-the-art telecommunication systems*
- *Earthquake-retrofitted buildings*

The community may need to invest in infrastructure, develop space to become more competitive in the business sector being targeted, and/or raise funds for incentives.

Business Attraction Activities

The five phases of business attraction are **preparation**, **targeting**, **marketing**, **sales**, and **closing the deal**.

PREPARATION

In every community, some business types fit the community goals better than others. The best results come from matching the profiles of business prospects with your community assets and vision. The following resources are available to assist you with these efforts:

Resources	*Ask For*
State Development Office	Targeting study
Electric or Gas Utility	Industries that complement available utilities
Railroad Agent	Industries that utilize rails to transport products
Manufacturers	Complementary industries and suppliers
Existing Businesses	Suppliers and partners
State Labor Office	Profile of existing labor market
Site Selector	Companies interested in existing community assets

TARGETING

Targeting gives you the greatest likelihood of meeting community goals. It is also a more effective use of your limited resources and helps you focus on specific business sectors:

Manufacturing —

- ▶ Has long been the foundation of economic development attraction efforts despite slow growth in industry.
- ▶ Jobs pay well and the industry is capital intensive.
- ▶ Results in higher tax revenues for local and state governments.
- ▶ Is considered a base industry, i.e., one that brings capital into the local economy from outside sources.

☼ SNAPSHOT ☼

100 manufacturing jobs can produce 315 additional related jobs.

Distribution —

- ▶ Offers the opportunity to create jobs without the need to upgrade the local infrastructure.
- ▶ Places little or no burden on the local infrastructure.
- ▶ Requires access to an interstate—something many rural communities have, but have not been able to leverage in the past.
- ▶ Wages are approximately equal to low-skilled manufacturing jobs.

Back-Office Operations —

- ▶ Deliver support services for many industries and businesses.
- ▶ Departments such as sales, marketing, collections and accounting, data processing, customer service, research, telemarketing, order processing, reservation centers, and claims processing are particularly suitable.
- ▶ Heavily reliant on high-quality telecommunications, particularly toll-free service, and locally available clerical workers.

☼ SNAPSHOT ☼

Business attraction generates 5 to 10% of the new jobs in a community.

High-Tech Research and Development —

- ▶ R & D facilities tend to pay their workers very well.
- ▶ Companies often separate their R & D activities because one area may have a competitive advantage due to either lifestyle choices or access to institutes of higher learning.
- ▶ Capital investment is less than many manufacturing facilities, but greater than distribution or back-office facilities.

Once you have targeted your business attraction program to one of these sectors, don't hesitate to focus dollars and effort even further by concentrating on specific companies. Use the following brief summary as a guide.

SECTOR	TYPE OF SITE	UTILITY NEEDS	TAXES	INCENTIVES	WORK FORCE	LINKS	TRANSPOR-TATION	FINANCE
MANUFACTURING	Usually single facility, can be as large as a campus	Electricity, water, natural gas	Large tax-payer	Occasionally required	Mixed between high- and low-skilled jobs	Many	Close to highway; easy access to airport	May take low-cost financing assistance, if offered
DISTRIBUTION	With "traffic"	Electricity	Medium level of tax revenue	Moderate requirements	Mostly low to moderate job skill levels	Usually few	Close to highway	Often have their own finance capabilities
BACK-OFFICE OPERATIONS	Centralized in labor market	May require excellent telecommunications support	Personal property tax revenue often greater than real estate tax revenue	Moderate requirements for incentives	Mostly low to moderate job skill levels	Many, due to labor-intensive nature of business	Not a large priority	May take low-cost financing assistance, if offered
RESEARCH & DEVELOPMENT	Scenic view or business park preferred	Very minimal	Proportionate to size of facility	Frequently do not qualify	High-skilled and clerical support	Usually few	Not a large priority	Often have their own finance capabilities

MARKETING:

In the business of business attraction, what you do can be as important as the decision to do it. It stands to reason that the more money an organization has to spend on any marketing technique, the more effective it becomes. The sample chart on the following page shows some of the key selling activities undertaken in business attraction. As you build your program, select those activities that make the best sense for your community, location, and budget.

☼ SNAPSHOTS ☼

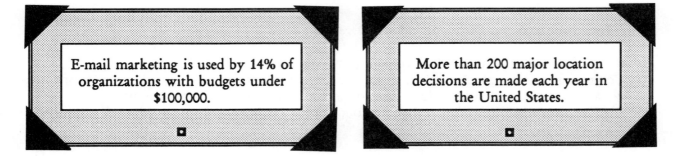

E-mail marketing is used by 14% of organizations with budgets under $100,000.

More than 200 major location decisions are made each year in the United States.

MARKETING STRATEGY	TARGET AUDIENCE	PARTNERS	RESOURCES	COST
Distribute Visitor Packets	Business people with overnight stays	Hotel owners, bed and breakfast operators	Community information cards	Low
Rediscover Graduates	Alumni from local schools	High school and college reunion committees	Coming home letters, mailing lists	Low
Join Associations	Targeted industry groups	Local businesses familiar with industry	Personnel to attend seminars	Low to moderate
Send Direct Mail	Targeted industry groups		Marketing lists, multiple mailing pieces	Moderate
Attend Trade Shows	Specific industry	Local businesses familiar with industry	Trade show booths, marketing materials	Moderate
Advertise in Magazines	Site selectors	Neighboring communities	Creative ad	High
Public Relations Campaign	Targeted industries	Journalists	Mailing list, media packets	Low

SALES:

If you want to identify the best prospect for the community, you have to get inside the mind of the business and find out why they would want to come to your area. Prospects make relocation decisions based on the WIIFME theory: *What's in it for ME?* Their priority is not to create jobs or sustain a community's economic health, but rather to generate a higher return on their investment. The six factors that most industrial firms consider are:

1. *Access to markets*
2. *An educated, skilled workforce*
3. *Ready, affordable industrial sites*
4. *High-quality infrastructure and amenities*
5. *Financing incentives*
6. *Friendly people with a pro-business attitude*

Most businesses that choose to relocate want to get their operations moved and started as soon as possible. When they're not working, they're not making money. The best chance of attracting a new employer is if you have a site that is:

▸ *readily available*
▸ *easily accessible*
▸ *"construction-ready"*

▸ *includes utilities and other necessary infrastructure*
▸ *priced correctly*

With these issues under control, you have an enhanced chance of making the "short list" of communities to be considered and of having a prospect visit your community.

CLOSING THE DEAL

Sooner or later, your community will need to consider using incentives to attract new businesses. Incentives are an important negotiating tool because they lower the cost of doing business. For most communities new to economic development, the use of incentives will require substantial leadership and education for the board member. Entire books have been written on the subject.

Some key points about incentives are:

☞ *They are a factor in most major relocation projects*
☞ *They can come from state or local governments or from the community itself.*
☞ *They are important for closing the deal and can be used to both party's advantage.*
☞ *They are negotiating tools, not entitlements.*
☞ *When used effectively, they create a win/win situation.*
☞ *Communities have much more at their disposal than they think.*

✿ SNAPSHOT ✿

Skills training assistance is the most frequently offered incentive by communities.

EXAMPLES OF COMMUNITY INCENTIVES

Workforce Assistance —   Hiring, training, relocation

Operating Assistance —   Frozen or reduced utility rates
Reduced taxes, abatements, and exemptions
Reduced site costs
Financing
Technical assistance
Permitting process assistance

Infrastructure Assistance —   Improvements to building or site
Improvements to public infrastructure
Utility extension or capacity expansion

BUSINESS ATTRACTION
DEVELOPMENT PLAN

Activity	Description	Champion	Budget	Start Date	End Date
Targeting	Identifying the types and location of companies to attract.				
	Measurement: Targeted businesses are classified by standard industrial codes (SIC), size, pay rate, etc.				
Promotion	Various types of printed material to be used in the campaign.				
	Measurement: Brochures designed, printed, and distributed.				
Activity - 1	Which attraction activity do you want to pursue? Select one that makes the best sense for your community.				
	Measurement: The most effective method of attraction is determined, and research is under way.				
Activity - 2	Activity:				
	Measurement:				
Activity - 3	Activity:				
	Measurement:				
Funding	Now that you know what you want to do, how are you going to pay for it?				
	Measurement: Funds are committed and for implementation phase.				
Implementation	Set a schedule for implementing your attraction plan.				
	Measurement: Activities are executed.				
Feedback and Evaluation	Allocate time and resources in your activities to evaluate your effectiveness.				
	Measurement: Successes and failures are evaluated.				

Business Attraction at a Glance

What can you expect to accomplish?

Success can be determined by:

- ❑ the number of jobs created
- ❑ the amount of dollars invested
- ❑ the number of companies attracted
- ❑ tax revenue generated

Who will do the work?

- ❑ Professional staff at the state, county, and/or regional levels
- ❑ Key state resource people for your area
- ❑ Community leaders and local business
- ❑ Utility economic development partners

How will you pay for these activities?

- ❑ Regional, county, and/or state funding
- ❑ Lease revenue from property owned or donated
- ❑ Private sector fund-raising efforts
- ❑ Revenue from committed sources, i.e., building permits, vehicle license renewals, sales taxes, etc.

What role does the board member play?

- ❑ Project oversight and guidance
- ❑ Assisting with prospect tours
- ❑ Offering use of sales representatives
- ❑ Financial support to annual fund-raising effort

What Success Looks Like

It had been six years since the plant closed. After dozens of disappointing leads and several unsuccessful prospect visits, Ed had finally recruited his first company, a manufacturer of electric toothbrushes. The company wanted to build a 10,000-square-foot plant at the edge of town and they wanted to hire 35 workers to start and have 65 employed within one year.

Ed believed this company was perfect for the town of Field. The CEO had grown up in the same area and graduated from a local state university before he moved to the East and started his business. Three years after start-up he won the Small Business Administration's "Entrepreneur of the Year" award.

Ed got the CEO's name from the university and wrote him a "Come Back to Field" letter. The CEO, a hiker and backpacker, had spent a lot of time in the area's remote and scenic locations. He was intrigued enough by Ed's letter to make a couple of trips to Field. He told Ed that if he could get some help with developing a workforce, while maintaining incremental growth and profitability, he'd be interested. Meanwhile, Ed had completed due diligence research on the company and discovered its growth potential.

Ed arranged a meeting with the CEO and head of the local community college. They agreed to establish classes to teach the workforce specific skills needed to produce the product. They would work at the college to begin with, then move on site to train on specific equipment at the plant.

Ed presented an economic impact analysis to the City Council and county commissioners. His analysis showed that if the county could help with some short-term tax deferrals, it would balance out within five years. And, while the city had already provided basic infrastructure to the site during the development stages, Ed's analysis indicated they would receive long-term benefits by providing additional upgrades at the site. The Port owned the property and, with Ed's help, negotiated a lease for the land and a build-to-suit building with an extension or buy option that would help the company get started without burying them, plus provide a balloon payment to the Port at a time they projected some increased costs for capital improvements. Everyone would win.

The business community pulled together to provide contacts, sources for raw materials, and suggestions for shipping that would save the new company money. The CEO and his management team already felt like part of the community.

All of the hard work had paid off. Ed was finally going to experience his first ground-breaking ceremony. There was something sweet in the air around Field—success.

REFERENCES

Clark, Cal. *101 Ideas on Economic Development.* Peoples Gas, 1994.

Economic Development Organization Survey Report: A Growth Strategies Organization Publication. Special Edition, 1998.

Forman, Maury, and James, Mooney. *The Race to Recruit.* Kendall/Hunt Publishing, Dubuque, Iowa, 1996.

Harding, Ford. *Rain Making.* Bob Adams, Inc., Publisher, Holbrook, MA, 1994.

Introduction to Economic Development. Council for Urban Economic Development, 1998.

Kotler, Philip, et al. *Marketing Places.* Free Press, 1993.

Lovorn, John. *100 Do's and Don'ts for Economic Developers.* The Pace Group, 1989.

Chapter 12:
START-UPS AND EMERGING ENTERPRISES

Guiding Principles:

☞ Developing start-ups and emerging enterprises can create more jobs than attracting one company.

☞ Development of start-up and emerging businesses may be the best strategy for communities with a creative spirit but limited resources.

☞ Legislative and policy issues can influence a community's success more than the community's desire to focus on entrepreneurial development.

☞ Training and one-on-one consulting are the most effective means of developing entrepreneurs and emerging businesses.

☞ Management, overhead, and micro-loans are the most important types of assistance for emerging enterprises.

☞ Small business incubators can effectively offset the high failure rates of entrepreneurs and emerging enterprises.

☞ An enterprise development strategy must include mentors or experts who can evaluate a business and assist in marketing and financial plans.

Betsy, the head of the branch library in Field, had worked there for 25 years. An avid reader, she loved talking to people about books. She had a wonderfully creative mind and had initiated a number of programs that brought more people into her branch than any other library in the county. She was well-respected throughout the state library circles, was often invited to be on committees, and frequently gave presentations to various groups and associations.

Ed had asked Betsy to speak to the economic development planning group about the library's resources for creating home-based businesses. Ever since the plant had closed, she had helped a lot of people find resources on starting a business, so she was somewhat familiar with the subject. But she wasn't sure what Ed meant by economic development. Was it just a fancy term for jobs, or was it something more than that?

One of Betsy's friends worked in the state economic development office, so she decided to call him and talk to him about her presentation. He told her that economic development was more than creating jobs—it was about generating wealth for an entire community. Home-based businesses, he said, were an important source of income and job creation for small, rural areas like Field. He even teased her, "Hey, Betsy, maybe you should think about doing some sort of business out of your home and start making some real money!"

What her friend did not know is that Betsy had been thinking of leaving the library. Twenty-five years was a long time at any job, and now that her son was in college she was looking for a new professional challenge. One of her passions was trying to locate hard-to-find books for her patrons. She also received calls from her colleagues all over the state asking for assistance in finding certain books. If she could devote more time to researching requests, she would be much more successful. But there was always too much to do at the library.

Maybe she could start a business that specialized in locating hard-to-find books. She felt that it was a service people would pay for, and she really believed that there was a strong market beyond Field. She imagined working out of her home in her pajamas tracking down classic and specialty books for her customers in the Internet.

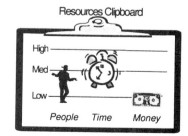

Resources Clipboard

High
Med
Low

People   Time   Money

She knew that starting a business was a dream of many people, but reading books about it and doing it were two different things. How would she market her services? And where would she get the money to upgrade her computer so she could increase her chances of locating books for people? What type of business entity would it be? What would her husband think of her leaving a secure job?

All these questions were on her mind as she began researching information for her presentation to the economic development planning group.

What are Start-ups and Emerging Enterprises?

America's greatest claim to fame in the hugely competitive global economy is that we lead the world in entrepreneurship and emerging enterprises. People in rural and urban areas can build major businesses from nothing but an idea. We produce more start-up enterprises in a month than European countries do in a year. While Fortune 500 companies have declined in job creation, entrepreneurs and emerging enterprises are creating jobs by the millions.

Start-up and emerging enterprise development stimulates the creative urge—or entrepreneurial spirit—of individuals who choose to be their own boss and have a product or idea they want to develop and market. Such individuals often need assistance in searching for more innovative ways to utilize available resources to create wealth. A start-up and emerging enterprise strategy helps people develop their managerial and technical skills. These entrepreneurs organize, operate, and assume the risk for business ventures either as a start-up (beginning) operation or as an emerging (two- to three-year-old) business.

Economic development organizations that focus on start-up and emerging enterprises help communities promote new business, rather than focus on outside risky business attraction efforts. This strategy requires high visibility in order to gain political and financial support. Nurturing entrepreneurial businesses from start-up through the various growth stages and into maturity requires a full-time effort and long-term commitment.

Why are Start-ups and Emerging Enterprises Important?

Source for Rural Jobs	Few other options are available for communities with no major industry or business attraction possibilities.
Creates Jobs	One small business will create, on average, 10 to 20 new jobs in a community.
Diversifies Local Economic Base	Reliance on a few industries could endanger a community's welfare during downturns in the economy. Multiple small businesses may keep it afloat.
Supports Local People	Home-grown firms typically remain in the community.
Enhances Local Tax Revenues	Successful entrepreneurs will provide additional income to the community.
Provide Role Models	Portrays positive image to youth, especially in rural communities.

CHARACTERISTICS OF ENTREPRENEURIAL DEVELOPMENT PROGRAMS

INNOVATIVE
Must design a program that meets the needs of the specific enterprises in the community.

FLEXIBLE
No two businesses are exactly alike, so the strategy must work for a variety of ventures.

CUT THROUGH RED TAPE
Start-ups and emerging businesses do not want to deal with bureaucracies that restrict them from getting their product to market.

LIMITED TIME
Start-ups and emerging businesses work with borrowed money so need assistance in a timely manner.

MODERATE COSTS
Expenses of training and technical assistance can be shared with other organizations.

GROWTH FOCUSED
Will be key to expansion projects in the future.

LONG-TERM
Assistance should continue from pre-start-up through growth and into maturity.

RISKY
There is a high failure ratio, because start-ups are long on ideas but short on management skills and financing.

Activities

The role of an economic development organization that focuses on small business development is primarily one of business and technical assistance. In order to succeed entrepreneurs and small businesses need MOM: **management assistance**, **overhead assistance**, and **micro-loan programs**.

Management Assistance

The number one reason that most businesses fail is due to poor management. Even though more books are on the market for entrepreneurs and emerging businesses than ever before, management is still the primary downfall of most start-ups. Books may be good for the dreamers, but one-on-one counseling assistance, including review of business and marketing plans, is essential for most people who want to succeed in reaching their dreams.

Economic development organizations need to be aware of all the available resources for start-ups and emerging businesses. Several excellent federal programs are:

FEDERAL ASSISTANCE PROGRAMS

Program	Primary Objective	Counseling	New Products	Technical Assistance	Business Financing/ Loan Assistance	Workforce Issues	Small Business Innovation Research
Small Business Administration	Aid, counsel, assist, and protect small business	X		X	X	X	X
Small Business Investment Corporation	Make equity investments and long-term loans				X		
Small Business Development Center	Provide business management and technical assistance	X		X	X	depends on local staff	
Innovation Assessment Center	Evaluate commercial viability of an invention		X				
Manufacturing Extension Partnership	Address critical and unique needs of small manufacturers	X	X	X		X	
Service Corps of Retired Executives	Match volunteers with small businesses for advice	X		X			
Trade Adjustment Assistance Centers	Provide assistance to work with at-risk businesses		X	X	X		
Procurement Technical Assistance Centers	Assist businesses in contracting with government agencies	X		X			

SOURCE: Ginger Rich, *Keeping Business Healthy, Happy and Local.* Seattle: Washington Department of Community Trade and Economic Development, 1998.

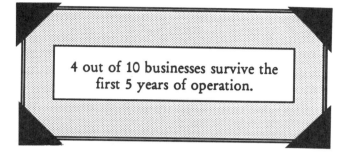

| 4 out of 10 businesses survive the first 5 years of operation. | People spent more than $500 million on business books in 1997. |

In addition to one-on-one counseling, the economic development organization should work with other groups to encourage entrepreneurial workshops and peer networking. SCORE, Small Business Development Centers, Small Business Administration, and community colleges are excellent partners in this endeavor. Since the goal of the workshops is to develop businesses and create jobs, the following questions should be asked before designing the course:

▶ *Is the course focused on start-ups or existing businesses?*

▶ *Does the program include academic knowledge and practical matters?*

▶ *Are the instructors well-versed in small business development?*

▶ *Is there a relationship or partnership with loan programs?*

▶ *Does the program have a relationship with an incubator program?*

▶ *Do the instructors provide follow-up assistance for students?*

▶ *Will experts in the field evaluate the business plan?*

▶ *Does the training lead to a marketable product?*

▶ *How is the training evaluated?*

Overhead Assistance

Many start-ups and emerging enterprises need a place from which to operate their businesses. They have three choices: their home, an incubator, or a rented facility. The decision usually depends on the type of company and the financial resources.

COMMUNITY	COST	ZONED FOR BUSINESS	SUPPORT SERVICES AVAILABLE
HOME	Low	Sometimes	No
INCUBATOR	Medium/High	Yes	Yes
RENTED FACILITY	Low	Yes	Rarely

HOME-BASED BUSINESSES

The phenomenal surge in home-based businesses in recent years can be attributed to recessions, corporate downsizing, certain industry upheaval, and peoples' desire to be their own boss. An economic development program that includes the promotion of home based business is a relatively inexpensive strategy for many small and rural communities.

✿ SNAPSHOTS ✿

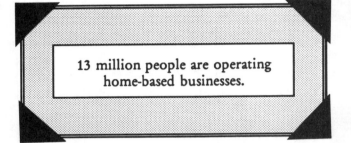

13 million people are operating home-based businesses.

Home-bases businesses create 8,219 new jobs each day.

INCUBATORS

Working at home, however, may not always be feasible. Many communities are looking at the possibilities of developing business incubators to satisfy their small business development needs. Incubators are multi-tenant facilities that have helped thousands of entrepreneurs and small businesses get started and have spawned more vibrant communities. Incubators provide start-up firms with low-cost space, low-cost shared services, proactive technical and management support, a peer network, and often financing assistance. Their success is measured in new jobs, economic diversification, the effect of new money in the economy, and real estate appreciation.

✿ SNAPSHOTS ✿

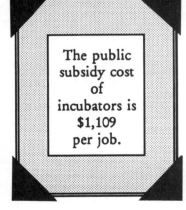

The public subsidy cost of incubators is $1,109 per job.

For every $1 of public money spent on incubators, the community's return on investment is $4.96.

84% of the graduates of incubators remain in their local communities.

The following table shows the stages of business evolution as well as the responsibilities of the people involved. Entrepreneurs and emerging enterprises should be nurtured in their start-up phase and monitored during their maturity stage.

STAGES OF EVOLUTION	AREAS OF RESPONSIBILITY		
	Stakeholders	Facility	Tenant Companies
Start-up	• Create core group of sponsors • Write a mission statement • Determine needs and resources of sponsors	• Perform cost/benefit analysis of building rehabilitation • Rehab initial space to be rented • Admit first tenant companies	• Provide basic shared tenant services • Offer flexible inexpensive space • Provide access to professional assistance
Business Development	• Enlist aid of sponsors to market facility • Enlist aid of sponsors to provide business support service • Expand base to include more stakeholders	• Attract one or more anchor tenants • Renovate space on an as-needed basis • Provide space for shared tenant service	• Assist company in capital acquisition • Create programs to encourage the mixing of companies • Market the collected products and services of tenants
Maturity	• Reassess levels of commitment to original plan • Evolve programs to reflect changing needs of stakeholders • Construct alliances between and among sponsors	• Manage cash flow • Construct specialized lease-hold components • Leverage physical plant for future interest opportunities	• Take equity in tenant companies • Subcontract to private service providers • Coordinate seed capital pool

SOURCE: Council for Urban Economic Development. Reprinted with permission.

MICRO-LOAN PROGRAMS

The world's hottest idea for reducing poverty has been the development of micro-credit loans. Eight million people in 43 countries are getting micro-credit loans. Though most of the loans are small, communities in the United States have expanded the idea of developing micro-loan and revolving loan programs.

Micro-loans and revolving loan funds (RLFs) are community-based financial institutions that provide access to capital for individuals and communities underserved by private financial institutions. They exist in every state and are supported by funders at all levels of government, as well as by private and philanthropic institutions. The institutions provide loans to start-ups and emerging enterprises that cannot attract private financing, and they recycle the repayments by re-lending the capital to other businesses. These loan programs are a flexible, effective tool for promoting business development, job creation, and economic self-sufficiency. The institutions have proven to be financially sustainable and collectively manage an estimated $8 billion in assets nationally.

✿ SNAPSHOTS ✿

> More than 300 micro-enterprise organizations now operate in the United States.

> Micro-enterprise programs have helped develop more than 50,000 businesses in the United States.

Just the Basics

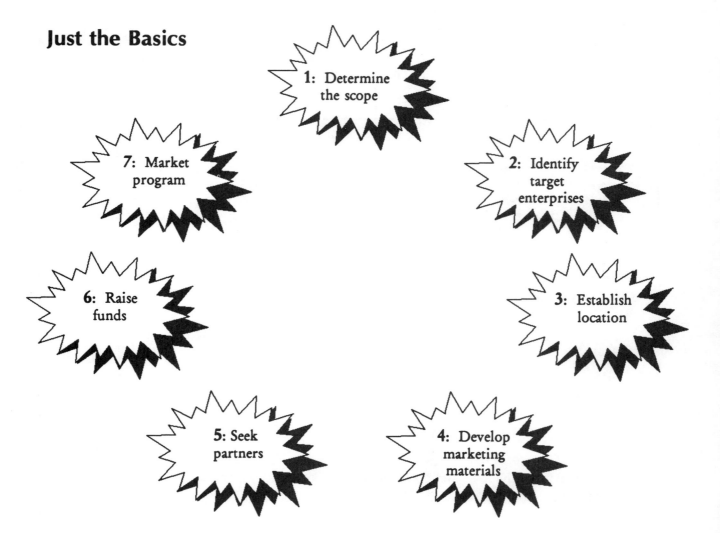

1: Determine the scope

2: Identify target enterprises

3: Establish location

4: Develop marketing materials

5: Seek partners

6: Raise funds

7: Market program

START-UPS AND
EMERGING ENTERPRISES PLAN

Activity	Description	Champion	Budget	Start Date	End Date
Needs Assessment	Identify the potential market for start-ups and emerging businesses.				
	Measurement: Home-based businesses and businesses two to three years old are documented.				
Reduce Barriers	Review legislation and policies that may affect start-ups and emerging businesses.				
	Measurement: Incentives and programs to encourage start-ups are developed.				
Plan Creation	Determine feasibility of incubator facility.				
	Measurement: Entrepreneurs, facility, and financing are available.				
Funding— Micro-Loan Program	Establish structure, appoint an oversight board, develop loan criteria, raise funds, and target enterprises.				
	Measurement: Micro-loan program created.				
Implementation	Coordinate technical assistance with partners.				
	Measurement: Cooperative working relationship established.				
Feedback and Evaluation	Develop criteria for success.				
	Measurement: Payback ratio is high, incubator is full, and companies are expanding on their own.				

Start-ups and Emerging Enterprises at a Glance

What can you expect to accomplish?

- ☐ Diverse enterprises
- ☐ Home-grown jobs
- ☐ Lower unemployment
- ☐ Future expansion possibilities

- ☐ Increase in community tax base
- ☐ Innovative and creative workforce

Who will do the work?

- ☐ Entrepreneurial trainers and educators
- ☐ Economic development staff knowledgeable in business management

- ☐ SBAs, SBDCs, and other management and technical assistance groups

How will you pay for these activities?

- ☐ Fee-for-service
- ☐ State grants

- ☐ Operational budget

What role does the board member play?

- ☐ Business referrals
- ☐ Oversight of micro-loan program

- ☐ Serve on board of an incubator
- ☐ Identify potential entrepreneurs

What Success Looks Like

It was a happy day for Betsy. She was graduating from the incubator and moving into her own facility. Her business, Search and Read, had blossomed over the last two years. She was making more money now than she ever did while working at the library. So many requests for books came in that she hired two part-time workers.

Moving into the incubator was one of the smartest decisions she had ever made. It really helped her survive during those first tough months while she was learning how to run a business. So many little costs kept adding up. For awhile, she thought if she had known about them before she began, she might not have even considered leaving the library.

Fortunately, for the first three months the space she used was rent-free, and after that she paid only a minimal amount. The incubator had several powerful computers that allowed her to do extensive research on hard-to-find books. More importantly, Ed offered some free classes on marketing a company, building a web site, and "looking small but acting big." The community college had a whole curriculum of other management courses, and she took advantage of all of them.

Betsy was now ready to go out on her own. Her web site had just won an award that generated a lot of publicity and a lot more business. She had received a micro-loan to buy several more computers and now was moving into an office park close to her home—something she had dreamed about for a long time.

She felt proud. No longer was she Betsy the librarian. Now she was Betsy the entrepreneur.

∞

REFERENCES AND RESOURCES

Black, Harry. *Achieving Economic Development Success.* International City Management Association, 1991.

Introduction to Economic Development. Council on Urban Economic Development, Washington, DC, 1998.

For more information on incubators, contact:

National Business Incubation Association
20 E Circle Drive, Suite 190
Athens, Ohio 45701
740-593-4331   *www.nbia.org.*

For more information on micro-lending, see:

America's Business Funding Directory
www.businessfinance.com

and

Lenders Interactive Services
www.lendersinteractive.com

Chapter 13:   TOURISM

Guiding Principles:

☞ Tourism can help diversify your economy.

☞ Leadership and a formal organization are needed to make your community a tourist destination.

☞ Your community may already have attractions that can draw visitors.

☞ Planning and evaluation of tourism are a continuous process.

☞ Community support is needed for tourism to be successful.

☞ Tourism may open the door to other economic development activities.

☞ Tourism is service oriented, thus making it labor-intensive.

☞ Tourism may require up-front investments from the public sector, such as improved buildings, roads, and other infrastructure.

Donna, the Continuing Education Coordinator at the community college in Field, was a newcomer to the economic development planning group. The dean had asked her to represent the school and she agreed, even though she had lived in Field for only five years. Since attending the planning group meetings, she had learned a lot and enjoyed participating in the future planning of the town.

Donna and her husband had just spent a long weekend with some old college friends. They had hiked to a beautiful waterfall in the woods, played a round of golf, rode their mountain bikes, and ate meals in a variety of restaurants. One afternoon they went "antiquing" and even tried roller-blading on a paved path around the lake. The Country Inn, where they were staying, was a delightful down-home kind of place located just a few blocks off the town's main street. Every night, the lounge at the Inn featured a very talented local comedian. Donna's party had a wonderful time. Before they left town, Donna talked with the Inn's managers and found out that the building had just been accepted on the National Register of Historic Places.

Donna wondered if Field could offer any of the same experiences as the area she had just visited. After all, the river was just outside of town, and they bordered a national forest. There were several decent restaurants in town, as well as a small hotel, a bed and breakfast, a couple of antique shops, and two golf courses in the area. And one vegetable gardener grew some awfully big pumpkins every year.

When Donna took her ideas to the next planning group meeting, they made a list of all of the town's "hidden treasures" that others might enjoy. They surprised themselves by how many there really were. A lot of those attractions, however, were not "visitor-friendly"—yet. They needed repair, enhancement, or just plain marketing. Fortunately, their main street was currently undergoing a badly needed facelift, and they talked about maps and marketing ideas to get people to come to Field.

They discussed at length whether tourism really fit their town and if it would be a good thing or a drain on existing resources. Would it generate higher-quality jobs? Would restoring the historic buildings cost more than they'd ever get back? Could the streets and parking lots accommodate an influx of visitors? They finally agreed to explore the whole topic and look at what other communities were doing.

Resources Clipboard

High
Med
Low

People   Time   Money

What is Tourism?

Tourism is a conglomeration of many different businesses—hotels, restaurants, gas stations, shops, museums, campgrounds, airlines, theme parks, rental car agencies, resorts. Each complement the other and are often interdependent on each other for success and survival.

In some ways, tourism is an intangible industry; it is not as easy to quantify or track as manufacturing. Yet travel and tourism is considered to be the second largest industry (behind health services) in terms of employment, accounting for more than 7 million jobs in 1997—a payroll of $127.8 billion. Travel and tourism in the United States generate an estimated $500 billion in expenditures every year.

Ten years ago, many cities, towns, regions, and states did not view tourism as an industry. Today, these areas are developing and promoting the industry and view it as an important part of their economy.

TYPES OF TOURISM

- ★ Outdoor Recreation
- ★ Sightseeing
- ★ Entertainment / Spectator Sports
- ★ Community Events and Festivals
- ★ Business Conventions and Conferences
- ★ Visits by Friends and Relatives

- ★ Historic and Cultural Activities
- ★ Hunting, Fishing, Wildlife Watching
- ★ Retreats and Weekend Workshops
- ★ Personal Business
- ★ Shopping
- ★ Passing through Communities

Why is Tourism Important?

Tourism can bring substantial benefits to a community and its residents. It is one of the few industries that brings new money into a community—that is, money from *outside* your boundaries. Tourist spending creates a chain reaction flowing through your local economy.

Diversifies the Economy	Helps communities be less reliant on one or two industries (e.g., lumber, fishing).
All Businesses Benefit	Visitors patronize hotels, resorts, campgrounds, and restaurants—as well as gas stations, grocery stores, pet shops, hardware stores, drugstores, gift shops, churches, etc.
Brings New Money	When a visitor spends money in your community, most of it stays and recirculates among local residents. Today's tourist may also be tomorrow's investor.
New Tax Dollars	All levels of government benefit from taxes paid by visitors.

Creates Jobs	Tourism is a stable, year-round industry in many communities and is a main source of employment in other areas during certain seasons (e.g., ski resorts, national parks).
Boosts Appearance	Communities often become more visually appealing in order to attract visitors.
Assists in Business Attraction	Industries prefer to locate in communities with tourist amenities.
Youth Opportunities	Part-time or seasonal jobs match employment needs of youth and second-wage earners.
Helps Support Community Facilities	Outside dollars are used to support amenities used by residents.

AREAS OF CONCERN

Your community has little control over whether visitors will come or not. But you can and should influence to what degree you develop tourism. Consider how the community may be impacted by the following issues:

Conflicts between residents and tourists — Visitors are often not familiar with the lay of the land in your area and may not respect the rights of private property owners. Careful design and community planning for visitor services and access can greatly help minimize aggravations.

Internal community conflicts — An industry–versus–the-rest-of-the-community attitude may develop, especially during the infancy stages of tourism development, and fester into antagonism or hostility.

Environmental pressures — More people may cause pollution, depletion, or deterioration of your area's natural resources.

Transient, low-wage workers — Many travel-oriented jobs are seasonal and entry level. Some rural areas with a small population base may need to find nonlocal employees to service the guests.

Public services — Roads, sewer, and safety (law enforcement, rescue teams, medical emergency assistance) may need to be upgraded or enhanced.

CHARACTERISTICS OF TOURISM PROGRAMS

MULTIPLIER EFFECT Many elements of a community gain indirectly or are influenced by an increase in dollars and people.	**HIGH IMPACT** Tourist programs and attractions create employment and bring new money into the economy.
DEVELOPS ENTREPRENEURS Spirit of small business is a major component of the tourism industry.	**COMPETITIVE** Thousands of communities compete for tourist dollars.
FLEXIBLE COSTS Volunteer organizations can generally operate with annual funding levels of $5,000 to $25,000.	**OPINION ORIENTED** Word-of-mouth is an important marketing technique and is dependent on the visitor's experience.
SERVICE ORIENTED Businesses must train employees to provide customer service to the public.	**ENTRY-LEVEL JOBS** Many of the jobs created are low paying and/or seasonal.

Assessing Your Community

What does your community have? What does it need?

Potential visitors are interested in a variety of things: unique sites, museums, shopping, parks, theater, and recreational opportunities. These items together are what make your community a *destination*.

Most communities don't have a *single* mega-attraction, something that by itself draws masses of visitors. In fact, most communities have a *number* of complementary attractions. Still others recognize that they are not year-round destinations so try to attract visitors for short periods of time or when visitors are passing through en route to a nearby destination.

The community tourism assessment process does not begin with the assumption that tourism *is* good for your community. Instead, it begins with the notion that tourism *may be* good for the area. After answering many of the questions below, a community may realize that a different economic development strategy would be more appropriate.

Assessing your community's existing attractions will aid you in developing and planning for any additional, needed attractions. Two questions to ask before you start are:

> ▶ *Is anyone interested in my community's attractions?*
> ▶ *What is our market potential?*

Factors that will influence your answers include:

Location   How many people are within a four-hour drive?
How many are within a day's drive?
Are you near any major metropolitan areas?

Access   Is your community easy to get to?
Are the highways in good condition?
Are the ferries or passenger trains to your community reliable?
Do alternative forms of transportation exist from metropolitan areas to your town?

Traffic Patterns   Do many people travel near or through your community?
Does the amount of traffic fluctuate during the year?

Competition   What are your neighboring communities doing?
How well are they doing it?

Attractions   Are your community's attractions interesting?
Are they convenient for travelers to visit?
Are they open during convenient hours? Seasonal?

Costs   Are tourist-related businesses in your community priced competitively?

Just the Basics

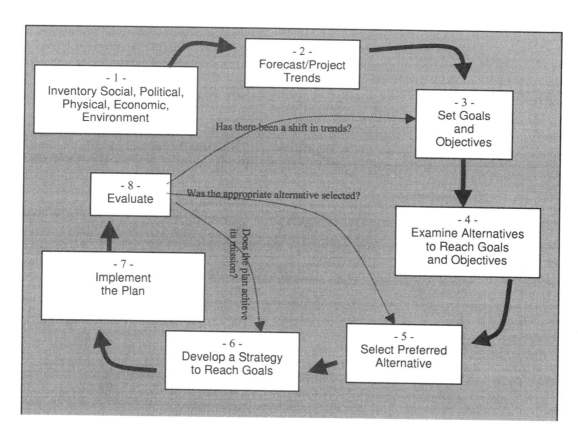

QUESTION	BENEFIT	CONCERNS
Is your community dependent upon one industry?	If yes, tourism could help diversify your economic base.	Additional infrastructure.
Are local businesses — expanding? — stable? — declining?	If stable or declining, tourism can provide a boost.	If declining, improvements may need to be undertaken.
Is unemployment seasonal?	If developing during the slack season, tourism may help.	Residents may resent congestion during their quiet time.
Are the unemployed — skilled? — unskilled?	Unskilled may benefit from an increased need for service workers with minimum skills. Skilled may be able to explore creative opportunities, such as entrepreneurial businesses.	Training may be needed for unskilled.
Is there an appropriate labor force available locally?	If yes, tourism can provide needed jobs.	If no, workers may need to be imported from other areas.
Have sales tax and other taxes such as bed tax revenues — increased? — declined? — remained stationary?	Increased revenues can reduce the burden on local residents. Increased funds will help pay for promotions, setting an upward spiral movement.	When revenue is not available, initial expenditures must first be made.
Is there a diversity of shops and stores?	If yes, then this is a drawing card for visitors.	If no, greater diversity may have to be encouraged which is difficult and requires extensive work.
Is your downtown or main street area — attractive? — in need of clean-up? — in need of restoration and repair?	Attractive towns have a greater potential for luring visitors. If clean-up is needed, ask volunteer organizations to help.	Funding is required for restoration and repairs.
Is your community receptive to increased tourism activity?	If yes, you have the local support needed to market your area.	If your community is not interested, you will need to do consensus building, which is time-consuming.
Are local cultural activities — thriving? — struggling? — top quality? — nonexistent?	If thriving or top quality, you can expand the audience attendance at these functions and offer a broader range of things to do.	If struggling or nonexistent, then time and money is needed to develop.
How many recreational activities does your community have? — not many — some, but they are difficult to find — many choices and great facilities	If you have many choices and great facilities, you have a gold mine! Not-easy-to-find ones can be an asset, once they are developed.	If there aren't many, there is little potential to attract visitors. Step back and look at your community through the eyes of an outsider.

TOURISM DEVELOPMENT PLAN

Activity	Description	Champion	Budget	Start Date	End Date
Organization	Identify who or what local group is going to get the ball rolling.				
	Measurement: Group established and meeting regularly.				
Local Involvement	Create broad community interest, foster volunteerism, and solicit input from local citizens.				
	Measurement: Community involvement and support for tourism are established.				
Attraction Development	Inventory and assess existing and potential attractions that could draw visitors to your community.				
	Measurement: A database of community assets and attractions is established.				
Community Appearance	Identify and implement community improvements.				
	Measurement: Capital investment by the public sector and tourism bureau is occurring.				
Visitor Services	What kind of reception services can be designed and implemented?				
	Measurement: Visitor information program implemented and functioning.				
Public Services	What public improvements are necessary to support tourism?				
	Measurement: Tourism-dependent issues are included in the capital improvement plan.				
Pre-Marketing	Develop a marketing plan, identify target markets to concentrate your efforts.				
	Measurement: Preliminary marketing data collected and ready for use.				
Funding	How will you fund your program? Are there visitor-related taxes in place? Are grants available?				
	Measurement: Funding secured for tourism effort.				
Marketing	Implement and evaluate your marketing plan.				
	Measurement: Action-oriented marketing plan in place.				
Feedback and Evaluation	Is the program being impartially reviewed and evaluated?				
	Measurement: Annual or biannual program review is executed.				

MEASUREMENTS OF SUCCESS

Your community's success in developing a tourism industry can be determined by the following:

EMPLOYMENT *Have new jobs been created?*

Are shops, museums, theaters, hotels, etc., hiring more employees to service the additional visitors coming to your area?

Has there been a decrease in your unemployment rate?

BUSINESS EXPANSION *Have new restaurants, hotels, shops, etc., opened since you started?*

Are there any plans to expand existing facilities?

Are any national franchises looking to expand into your area?

LODGING **Number of rooms available in hotels, motels, bed and breakfasts, etc.:**

How many did you have before you actively sought visitors?
How many do you have now?
Do you still need more rooms because the demand is so great?

The average daily rate (ADR) of your lodging properties:

What was this before you began, and what is it now?

The occupancy percentage at local lodging properties:

Is it in line with neighboring communities?

✿ SNAPSHOTS ✿

Worldwide, tourism employs more than 204 million people.	Local, state, and federal tax revenues from the tourism industry are more than $54 billion annually.

Tourism Development at a Glance

What can you expect to accomplish?

- ❏ Determination of whether tourism is suitable for your community
- ❏ Development strategies for encouraging tourism
- ❏ Coordination between people involved with your gateway program and new resident attraction program

Who will do the work?

- ❏ Professional organization: a visitors bureau or chamber of commerce
- ❏ Community leaders
- ❏ Local businesses
- ❏ Volunteers

How will you pay for these activities?

- ❏ Local visitor-related taxes: hotel/motel tax, fuel tax
- ❏ Donations and gifts
- ❏ Grants, endowments, or other special funding
- ❏ Festivals and events license fees
- ❏ General fund revenues
- ❏ Advertising sales in tourist publications

What role does the board member play?

- ❏ Assists in preparing the plan
- ❏ Networks with local business leaders to promote tourism
- ❏ Assists in identifying and securing funding
- ❏ Acts as ambassador while in other towns or cities to encourage visitors to your community

What Success Looks Like

As Donna walked down the main street of Field, she was happy to see all the people in the shops and restaurants. A bus full of out-of-state visitors was pulling up to attend the opening of the dinner theater. As she walked a little farther, she saw the historical society setting up in the park for Saturday's Heritage Festival.

Donna couldn't believe how alive the town had become—families and couples strolling through the streets and stores, people lining up to go to the theater. She remembered her friends and their long weekend getaway and thought, "Now we don't have to go so far away—we have it all here!"

REFERENCES

Amos, Carole J., and Thomas D. Park. *Hometown Discovery: A Development Process for Tourism.* Cooperative Extension Service, Clemson University, 1991.

Brooks, Roger. *Community Tourism Development Kit* (draft). Washington Department of Community, Trade and Economic Development, Tourism Development Division, 1998.

Dervaes, Claudine. *The Travel Dictionary.* Solitaire Publishing, 1996.

Gartrell, Richard B. *Destination Marketing.* Kendall/Hunt Publishing, Dubuque, Iowa, 1994.

Koth, Barbara, Glen Kreag, and John Sem. *Rural Tourism Development Project Training Guide.* Minnesota Extension Service, University of Minnesota, 1991.

Nuckolls, Jonelle, and Patrick Long. *Organizing Resources for Tourism Development in Rural Areas.* University of Colorado, Boulder, 1993.

Sustainable Tourism Development: Guide for Local Planners. World Tourism Organization, 1993.

Tourism USA. University of Missouri–Columbia, Department of Parks and Recreation and Tourism, 1991.

SECTION V.

WORKFORCE DEVELOPMENT

WORKFORCE DEVELOPMENT

Connie, the English instructor at Field High School for the past 17 years, had just returned home from the five-year reunion of Field's 1995 graduating class. That was the year she had won the state's "Best Teacher" award. She was glad to see all of her old students, but at the same time she was disturbed by what she had found.

Quite a few of her students had chosen not to go to college, but instead found jobs right after they graduated. Some had taken jobs at the plant, but now that the plant was closed they were unemployed. Others had found employment outside of Field, but they seemed to be low-wage jobs that required few skills. By her estimate, only 10 percent of the graduating class went on to college, and only half of them had gotten degrees. This was much different than her graduating class of 30 years ago, when 90 percent attended college and 80 percent graduated.

She began to question whether the Field educational system was preparing its students adequately. Were they churning out students just like the plant had produced a product? The plant was now gone because the managers had not kept up with the times. Could the school be far behind? She knew it had been awhile since she had changed her own curriculum, and she felt sure that was true for her colleagues as well. They were still teaching their students under the assumption that most would go to college.

Several weeks earlier, Ed had asked Connie to join the economic development group. She respectfully declined, as she was already on several other committees. And frankly, she didn't see what economic development had to do with teaching high school students. But now she decided to call Ed and ask if she could attend a meeting to get a better understanding of what economic development was and how it related to education.

At the meeting, she discovered that companies were hesitant to move to Field because they considered the workforce inadequate. A number of businesses had already moved because they couldn't find people who had basic

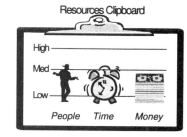

Resources Clipboard

High / Med / Low — People, Time, Money

skills, such as solving structured problems, working in groups, writing error-free letters, or doing simple tasks on a computer like word processing.

Connie was shocked. She had no idea that businesses were dissatisfied with the quality of the educational system. She immediately went back to her school and called a meeting of her fellow teachers to discuss what she had learned.

What is Workforce Development?

Workforce development is a statewide system of education and training that prepares people for high-skill jobs and assures employers of a skilled flexible workforce in the future. This comprehensive program is designed to improve the productivity level of the workers and allow companies to grow in the future. While the program may be articulated under a single organization (often the economic development office), it is actually implemented by a number of organizations throughout the community.

A workforce development effort can only succeed when it has the resources—qualified workers—to fill the jobs that new employers will have. It does little good to create jobs for which there are no people who can do them.

Workforce development includes:

Education reform—adjusting the local education system to produce graduates who have skills necessary for the next century.

Skill development for displaced workers—making sure that people who have lost their jobs never have it happen again due to their job skills.

On-the-job training—to help workers to gain new skills and handle the increasing use of technology in the workplace.

Welfare-to-work programs—to help people become economically self-sufficient by removing barriers, building skills, and meeting the individual's basic needs.

Because of the large number of individuals and organizations, the need for system-wide coordination and accountability in workforce development programs is substantial. While few agencies absolutely have to work together, the primary role of the economic development organization is to act as an intermediary and create a community-wide vision, so that everyone is recognized for their contributions and is provided an environment where they benefit from participation.

Why is Workforce Development Important?

Increases Productivity	The rate of worker productivity—the amount of work produced per unit time—has been steadily declining in the United States. Workforce development intends to reverse that trend.
Enhances Ability to Compete	A skilled workforce helps companies expand and remain competitive.
Fewer Entry-Level Positions	An expected decline in the number of young workers may lead to labor skill shortages in all professions.
Low-Skill Jobs are Disappearing	They will be replaced by jobs requiring a higher level of technical skill, especially with computers.
The Workforce is Aging	Without effective training, older workers could become entrenched in old ways, unwilling or unable to learn the new.
Opportunities for Women and Minorities	People historically denied higher-paying jobs will require more education and training. Women now make up nearly 50 percent of the workforce, and 65 percent of the entrants into the labor market will be women and minorities.
Aids in Retention of Workers	A trained workforce will lead to steady jobs, which will encourage their families to stay in the community.
Increases Standard of Living	Better job skills will lead to increased wages and upward mobility.
Reduces Illiteracy	Skill-building will enhance the self-esteem of the workforce, which will increase productivity.
Reduces Gap Between the Haves and Have-Nots	Skill shortages contribute to economic disparities between people in many communities. Workforce development helps balance the scale.

CHARACTERISTICS OF
WORKFORCE DEVELOPMENT PROGRAMS

COOPERATIVE
Workforce development occurs when a number of public agencies and private companies with similar goals and objectives enter into structured partnerships.

GRASS ROOTS
Problems with a local workforce can be solved from the bottom up, as opposed to top-down requirements essential to other economic development efforts.

CUSTOMER-DRIVEN
The type of workforce development effort you choose is highly dependent upon your local population and your community's strategic plan for future attraction.

LOCALLY FOCUSED
Your program will be specifically geared toward the needs of the community. National programs are merely resources for your local efforts.

ALL-INCLUSIVE
Workforce development affects all ages of the population: children in day-care, students in school-based learning programs, and young and older employees who need skills training.

EMPHASIS ON A MULTITUDE OF SKILLS
Workers will need the basic skills of reading, writing, and computation, as well as critical thinking and communication skills.

PROVIDE SUPPORT SERVICES
Career counseling, childcare, transportation, and financial aid should be made available to those who need them.

COORDINATED
Education and training must align private sector training, social services, and other services and with economic development strategies.

COMPETENCY-BASED
Students must be able to master the skills needed to find suitable and available jobs.

ACCOUNTABLE FOR RESULTS
The purpose of education and training is to get a good job, not just to be trained.

✿ SNAPSHOT ✿

More than 1 in 5 American adults cannot read a newspaper, compute with fractions or decimals, or find a street section on a map.

The Workforce of Today and Tomorrow

Programs to develop a strong workforce are usually presented in three clusters:

Youth
Adults
Adults with Barriers to Employment

The greatest number of new job opportunities will be in occupations that require some post-secondary education, but not a four-year degree from a college or university. If the supply of skilled workers is limited, a community's future economic growth could be constrained. Shortages in some professions may develop which will put additional hardships on rural areas that can least afford to lose jobs.

YOUTH

School-to-Work Programs: These programs establish a framework for the development of a comprehensive system that prepares young people for a high-skill, high-wage economy. The programs—which number in the thousands across the country—integrate school-based learning at high school with structured learning experiences in the workplace. They require partnerships with employers, educational institutions, and community-based organizations.

The School-to-Work Opportunities Act of 1964 provides funds to states and regions that establish school-to-work programs. All programs must include:

▶ *Work-based learning*
▶ *School-based learning*
▶ *Connecting activities between employers, schools, and students*

Employers need to see the benefits and opportunities that exist for their companies rather than the barriers. In most cases, this means the program must have a positive impact on the company's bottom line. At the same time, educators must realize curriculums cannot be developed with the intention that their students will move on to receive a four-year degree. Economic development organizations that choose to become intermediaries must reduce the burdens in terms of costs (financially and timewise) that employers and educators often experience in working with new programs.

✿ **SNAPSHOTS** ✿

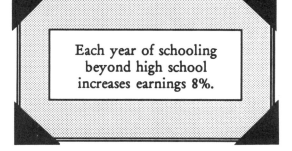

Each year of schooling
beyond high school
increases earnings 8%.

24% of companies with 20 to 99
employees are involved in some form of
school-to-work program.

SCHOOL-TO-WORK PROGRAMS

Goals of School-to-Work Programs	Employer Recruitment Strategies	Economic Development Organization Role	Public School Activities	Employer Activities

• Prepare students who do not attend 4-year colleges
• Address pressing labor needs
• Enrich high school education in areas of skill shortages
• Cultivate next generation of skilled workers
• Learning is organized around career majors
	• Emphasize programs that serve corporate and community goals
	• Identify private sector champion to recruit other employers
	• Target employers who:
	  – Experience skill shortages
	  – Operate in international markets
	  – Invest in education and training
	  – Have a history of community involvement
	• Build from relationships that already exist
		• Act as intermediary
		• Appoint representative steering committee
		• Administer program
		• Communicate and clarify expectations
		• Broker agreements with labor unions
		• Administer student paychecks
		• Establish and maintain credibility
		• Secure outside funding
		• Facilitate problems or miscommunications
			• Provide counseling
			• Match students with employers
			• Design or sponsor career days
			• Create curriculum with employer
			• Provide job assistance
			• Integrate work-based learning with academic classes
			• Offer a retraining guarantee to employers
				• Provide funding
				• Create curriculum with school
				• Establish type of program:
				  – Workplace mentors
				  – Career shadowing
				  – Internships
				  – Youth apprenticeships
				  – School visits from businesses
				• Train supervisors
				• Establish training standards
				• Create jobs for graduates

SOURCE: Developed from "Employer Participation in the School-to-Work Transition," by Erin Flynn, *Commentary*, Spring 1994.

Youth Entrepreneurship Programs: In some rural areas, starting a business is closer to a pipe dream than reality because of the lack of opportunities for young people to learn about running a business. This is a major contributor to the migration of young people away from rural areas. But numerous programs and camps all over the United States teach youth the elements of starting a business. Entrepreneurship can also be incorporated into the basic courses rather than taught as an entirely new curriculum.

✿ SNAPSHOTS ✿

7 out of 10 high school students want to start or own their own business.

90% of high school graduates surveyed rated their knowledge of entrepreneurship as poor.

High School Curriculum Tips: While economic development agencies cannot design curriculums for the schools, they can encourage instructors to incorporate skill-building activities as a way to enhance students' awareness of economic and employment issues, as well as encourage their entrepreneurial spirit.

Math:
Balance a checkbook
Prepare personal income financial statements and/or profit-and-loss statements and balance sheets for a fictitious business

English:
Write a press release or marketing brochure
Compose business letters
Read management books and write a report

History:
Study how inventions that changed the world came into marketplace
Read a biography on industrial leaders, a corporate history, or articles about local companies or individuals who were considered successful in business

Political Science:
Track how a particular legislative action affected small businesses in your area
Study the manufacturing and employment practices of a particular company in the global economy (e.g., sports shoe or soft drink manufacturers)

Science:
Identify and study companies or institutions that conduct research and development on particular products or methods.
Take a field trip to the testing laboratory of a nearby company

Economics:
Study the demographics of your own community
Calculate the amount of money spent by students (class or entire school) in one week and show where the money went in the form of pie charts, graphs, or other visual aids.

ADULTS

Training and Skill Development Programs: State and federal government agencies and the private sector share responsibility for much of the training and skill development of our workforce. These entities include:

- ▶ *Vocational and technical schools*
- ▶ *Community colleges*
- ▶ *Service delivery areas under the Job Partnership Act*
- ▶ *State-run employment services*
- ▶ *Apprenticeship programs*
- ▶ *Employer-provided training*
- ▶ *Worker retraining programs*
- ▶ *Job skills programs*

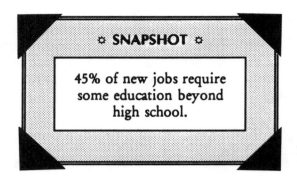

Beyond high school, the educational system must be able to produce qualified workers with skills that match employers needs. In order to do this, training and skill development must be able to adapt to the changing times.

Then:	Now:
Perform simple tasks	*Use complex technology and processes*
Follow instructions	*Solve problems*
Repeat same tasks	*Meet individual customer needs*
Work independently	*Work in teams*
Wait for improvements	*Identify ways to reduce production time*

However, despite the abundance of education and training entities, associations from all over the country are reporting that, due to a shortage of qualified workers, jobs are going unfilled, businesses are losing money, and productivity is declining.

Training is useless unless skills are developed to meet a company's current and future needs and it awakens people to their own intellectual strengths and weaknesses. Revamping the investment in training and skill development beyond high school will benefit everyone:

Industry: *Becomes more competitive*
Becomes a better customer of education system
Improves workforce skills across industry, including suppliers

Employers: *Increases return on training investment*
Improves hiring and performance assessment
Boosts workforce performance

Workers: *Ensures long-term employability*
Improves training and education decisions
Get skills recognized

Educators *Understand customer requirements*
and Trainers: *Develop better curriculum and training programs*
Strengthen relationships with local companies

Once again, the role of the economic development organization and its board is limited but crucial. They can act as the intermediary and coordinate meetings between company managers and educational entities. They can also make sure that the community strategic plan is in line with the needs of its businesses and citizen skills. Only then will employees be able to find top-quality jobs, and companies will increase sales and productivity.

ADULTS WITH BARRIERS TO EMPLOYMENT

Welfare-to-Work Programs: A strong economy has created a strong labor demand and increased the job availability for welfare recipients. Economic development practitioners have played an important intermediary role in connecting recipients with employers. Employers have received entry level and semiskilled workers and millions of people have acquired job skills and career opportunities. The states and federal government have created a number of programs to help individuals remove barriers, meet basic needs, and build skills.

People in the welfare system are generally divided into three tiers:

	CHARACTERISTICS	INVESTMENT	STRATEGIES
TIER 1	Some work skills In and out of workforce	Minimum	Short-term
TIER 2	Willing to work Little experience Need skill development	Medium	Medium Requires training and follow-up
TIER 3	Unwilling to work No experience Needs basic skills Needs training	High	Long-term Requires regular intervention and support

Many people in the first tier were hired early in the welfare reform movement. The challenge for economic development practitioners is to determine what it will take to move people now in the second and third tiers into the workforce during periods of economic prosperity. In most cases, this will require meeting basic needs, removing barriers, and building skills of those individuals.

A number of social service agencies will take the lead in meeting those requirements. The economic development group should focus on making businesses familiar with programs that will ease the burden of hiring people who have been on welfare. These include tax credits, wage subsidies, and training and screening programs offered by government agencies. These resources are particularly valuable in rural areas where a proportionately larger percentage of the residents receive public assistance benefits, have higher unemployment rates, and have fewer economic opportunities than the state's urban areas.

Nonprofit Enterprises: Nonprofit agencies are beginning to realize that they play an important part in economic development, as they have direct access to an untapped market of potential workers. They are also recognizing the need to identify other financial resources to maintain their organization's efforts in removing barriers and building the skill level of their clients.

Nonprofit enterprises—sometimes referred to as social purpose businesses, community-based businesses, or community wealth enterprises—are revenue-generating ventures founded to create jobs or training opportunities for hard-to-employ individuals. The job training activities support the venture operations that provide income, which in turn provides money for new training opportunities. People and corporations are eager to do business with companies that have a social purpose as well as provide quality goods and services.

The economic development organization must put on its business development hat and work with the nonprofit to establish whether the businesses is a well thought out idea and based on realistic assumptions. The economic development organization has to evaluate a nonprofit venture, just as it would any other small business request for assistance, and not be swayed by good intentions, but instead by good economics.

KEY INTERVENTIONS FOR HARD-TO-EMPLOY INDIVIDUALS

MEETING BASIC NEEDS	REMOVING BARRIERS	BUILDING SKILLS	PROMOTING ECONOMIC DEVELOPMENT
Physical Security	Childcare	Life skills	Job creation/ retention
• Food	Work-related costs	Language training	Self-employment
• Housing and utilities			
• Clothing		Literacy/ numeracy	Access to capital
• Clean water and sanitation	Health-related costs		
• Protection from violence and abuse		Job search	Technical assistance
	Disability-related costs	Academic upgrading	
Health/Mental Health			
• Health care services	Skills accreditation	Job training	
• Early childhood development			
• Self-esteem and support	Transportation		
• Counseling and mental health services			
• Substance abuse services			

SOURCE: Sherri Torjman, "How Can Communities Reduce Poverty," *Making Waves*, Centre for Community Enterprise, Summer 1998.

Just the Basics

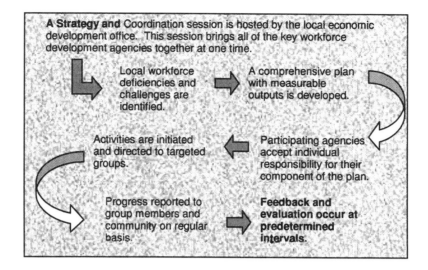

WORKFORCE DEVELOPMENT PLAN

Activity	Description	Champion	Budget	Start Date	End Date
Needs Assessment	Meet with local human resource directors to determine workforce development needs.				
	Measurement: Assessment is completed.				
Strategy Meeting	Organize a joint meeting of all workforce development agencies to coordinate service provision activities.				
	Measurement: Meeting is held and activities discussed.				
Plan Creation	Focus effort to match needs and resources for developing the area's workforce.				
	Measurement: Plans developed.				
Funding	Secure any necessary funding to assist with overall plan writing, publication, and coordination.				
	Measurement: Money is in the bank.				
Implementation	Set a schedule for implementing your attraction plan.				
	Measurement: Plan is implemented.				
Feedback and Evaluation	Allocate time and resources in your activities to evaluate your effectiveness.				
	Measurement: Evaluation completed.				

Workforce Development at a Glance

What can you expect to accomplish?

- Fewer people on the area's welfare roles
- Increased numbers of children in qualified day-care programs
- Lower unemployment rates
- Increased utilization of technology by the local workforce
- Educational system that combines technical skills learning with soft skills
- Increased retention of employees
- Improved recruitment of employees for businesses
- Increased productivity
- Educators, businesses, and community groups working together

Who will do the work?

- Trainers and educators who are part of the various service-providing agencies
- Economic development staff charged with coordinating the efforts
- Childcare service providers
- Managers who assist in training and curriculum development

How will you pay for these activities?

- State and federal funding
- Business sector funding available, if awareness and sensitivity is present
- Economic development program general fund dollars may be appropriated, if justified

What role does the board member play?

- Project oversight and guidance
- Assisting with strategy development
- Become a private sector champion to recruit other employers to school-to-work programs
- Become a role model by providing opportunities to welfare individuals
- Help establish organization as an intermediary by building on existing relationships among employers, educators, and community
- Identify curriculum experts in field of expertise

What Success Looks Like

Connie returned home from the five-year high school reunion of the Class of 2000. It was a wonderful evening. She had seen many of her old students and was very proud of them. Although the number of people who had graduated from college hadn't increased over that of the Class of '95, it seemed like more had skilled jobs with high wages. A few had even started their own businesses in Field right after high school and were quite successful.

When Connie joined the economic development group, she discovered how much education was linked to workforce. Shortly after the first meeting she attended, she and her colleagues began a series of meetings with employers in the area and community college representatives from a nearby town. Ed facilitated the meetings, and they discussed what skills would be necessary in order for their companies to grow. Many of the skills pertained to production activities for manufacturing, but employers also talked about basic business skills.

Connie made all sorts of changes to her curriculum to make it more relevant to her students' futures. She taught them how to write business letters and how to prepare marketing brochures and ad copy. She assigned them to read a biography on a businessperson who made a difference in the 20th century, as well as a book on business management. Connie and the math teacher worked with one class who developed an entire business plan for a day-care center business. Three years later, that business had four companies on contract. She also initiated a school-to-work program in which several students were interns for local employers, while others worked on marketing projects to promote local companies.

The community colleges also started collaborating with companies involved in manufacturing. Managers established standards and worked with instructors to design programs that fit their needs. Many jobs were created through this program.

Thanks to Ed and others in the economic development planning group, the whole school got involved in skill-building programs and school-to-work activities. More students were staying in Field after graduation and raising families. Connie felt as if she were a part of each student's success and looked forward to the next year's reunion.

REFERENCES

ED Handbook. California Association for Local Economic Development, League of California Cities, Sacramento, CA, 1997.

Emerson, Jed, editor. *New Social Entrepreneurs: The Success, Challenge, and Lessons of Non-Profit Enterprise Creation.* The Roberts Foundation, 1996.

Flynn, Erin. "Employer Participation in the School to Work Transition," *Commentary,* Spring 1994.

High Skills, High Wages. Washington Training and Education Coordination Board, Olympia, WA, 1998.

Introduction to Economic Development. Council on Urban Economic Development, Washington, D.C., 1998.

The Rural View on Welfare Reform. Washington State Rural Development Council, 1997.

Torjman, Sherri. "How Can Communities Reduce Poverty," *Making Waves,* Centre for Community Enterprise, Summer 1998.

SECTION VI.

DECISION

Chapter 15

DECISION TIME

Guiding Principles:

☞ Recognize and understand the unique assets of your community.

☞ Develop an economic development plan that matches the community vision.

☞ Pay attention to existing businesses.

☞ Maintain and upgrade infrastructure.

☞ Create a capacity for broad-based civic responsibility.

☞ Form partnerships to further community and regional goals.

☞ Protect resources and ensure high-quality development.

☞ Act on opportunities rather than reacting to problems.

☞ Develop reasonable time frames and measures of success.

☞ Communicate plans to community in a regular and timely manner.

☞ Provide funding for a 3- to 5-year period.

☞ Diversify the economy.

☞ Create a business-friendly environment.

☞ Do not mortgage the community's future.

The time had finally come to make some hard decisions about the future of Field.
For the last six months, Ed had been working with members of the planning group to learn everything there was to know about the community. They had looked at Field as an alien from another planet would have looked at it. They asked questions, made inventory lists, and interviewed people.

During that period, Ed and some members of the group also attended some excellent introductory workshops sponsored by the American Economic Development Council and the Council for Urban Economic Development. They brought back materials with examples of economic development strategies being used by other communities in similar situations. They shared this information with the mayor and the rest of their colleagues.

Now Mayor Rose was calling a meeting to decide on a direction for the town. They were ready to match their vision with their resources. They were ready to tell the outside world about Field.

The previous chapters gave you an overview of what the broad world of economic development is about. Now, you need to decide what the future of your community may look like. In order to do that, you need to answer the question, "What is the vision we hold for our community?" Here are four scenarios:

Bedroom Community/No Growth—This community has decided it does not want new commercial or industrial growth. It wants to stay its current size and not actively attract new residents, businesses, or industry. It realizes that this decision has a ramification that must be accepted: the lack of increase in tax base will result in higher tax rates in order to maintain the same standard of living for this community.

Bedroom Community/Residential Growth—This community wants to attract new people. Those people should be residents who will live and shop locally. Business and industrial growth is not a priority for this community.

Tourism/Commercial Community—This community is seeking to capture retail activity from shoppers or tourists who visit the community and reside elsewhere. The amount of tax revenue attainable from these activities will meet the budget goals of this community. Industrial growth is not a priority.

Business/Industrial Point of Destination—This community wants to be the employment center of the region. They desire to attract new business and industrial investment on an ongoing basis. Their goal is to reap the tax benefits of commercial and industrial investment while also minimizing work commutes for current residents.

Before you make your decision, let's review the resource requirements of each scenario we've developed in this workbook.

Table 1 – Resource Summary

PROGRAM	PEOPLE	TIME	MONEY
Infrastructure	Low	High	High
Downtown Revitalization	High	High	Medium
Gateway Programs	Low	Low	Low
Business Parks	Medium	High	High
Spec Building Development	Medium	High	High
New Resident Attraction	High	Medium	Low
Partnerships	High	Medium	Low
Business Retention and Expansion (BRE)	High	Medium	Medium
Business Attraction	Medium	High	High
Start-ups and Emerging Enterprises	Low-Medium	Medium-High	Low-Medium
Tourism	Medium	Medium	Low
Workforce	Medium	Medium	Medium

Next, look at the four scenarios above and see which economic development program is most applicable to your community. In Table 2, we've used the qualifiers of rarely, marginal, better, and best. Here's what they mean:

Rarely: This program is not applicable for this scenario in the vast majority of situations.

Marginal: This program has some applicability to this scenario, but it probably has a lower priority than other options.

Better: This program is applicable to this scenario and should probably be weighted in the middle of the pack of your priorities.

Best: This program is well-suited to this scenario and should be at the top of your priorities.

Table 2 — Focusing the Vision				
PROGRAM	BEDROOM— NO GROWTH	BEDROOM— RESIDENTIAL	TOURISM / COMMERCIAL	BUSINESS / INDUSTRIAL
Infrastructure	Marginal	Marginal	Better	Best
Downtown Revitalization	Marginal	Better	Best	Best
Gateway Programs	Rarely	Marginal	Better	Best
Business Parks	Rarely	Rarely	Rarely	Best
Spec Buildings	Rarely	Rarely	Marginal	Best
New Resident Attraction	Rarely	Better	Better	Best
Partnerships	Rarely	Marginal	Best	Best
BRE	Rarely	Better	Better	Best
Business Attraction	Rarely	Rarely	Marginal	Best
Start-ups	Rarely	Marginal	Best	Better
Tourism	Rarely	Better	Best	Better
Workforce	Marginal	Rarely	Best	Best

Now let's organize your economic development strategy. In Table 3, write the vision you hold for your community that best matches one of the four scenarios (Bedroom, Residential, Tourism/Commercial, or Business/ Industrial) at the top of the chart. Then, using Table 2, rank the economic development program(s) that best apply to your community in the boxes to the right. First indicate those that fit best, then those ranked as "better," and so on, until you get to the lowest-ranked program.

After each program is ranked, prioritize them to fit your community. The most important program would be given the first priority, the next-most important would be given second priority, and so on, until you've worked through the list of alternatives. As you do this step, keep in mind the amount of resources required for each program (see Table 1 — Resource Summary).

Table 3 — Setting the Course of Action

YOUR COMMUNITY

COMMUNITY VISION: _____	Rank	Priority
Program #1		
Program #2		
Program #3		
Program #4		
Program #5		
Program #6		
Program #7		
Program #8		
Program #9		
Program #10		

PUTTING IT ALL TOGETHER

Now let's estimate how much money your community will commit to various economic development efforts. Also acknowledge that the project will have a direct impact on the amount of funds you'll be able to generate. Then determine how much money you think your community will raise on an annual basis.

In Chapter 2, "Establishing an Economic Development Organization," we pointed out that the average capital commitment at the county level is $3 per county resident. If your county is ready to step up to the table, your figure may be twice that (or more!). If you're just beginning, it may be something less. So go ahead and guesstimate what the annual budget for economic development activities in your community may be:

Table 4 — Estimated Annual Commitment for Economic Development	
YOUR COMMUNITY	SAMPLE CHART
$	**$125,000**

Now organize your efforts according to the priorities you established in Table 3—Setting a Course of Action. After each priority, estimate how much money you think your community will commit to the respective effort. Make sure you do not exceed the annual commitment identified in Table 4.

Table 5 — Budgeting				
YOUR COMMUNITY			**SAMPLE CHART**	
VISION:			*TOURISM / COMMERCIAL*	
	Title	Budget	Title	Budget
Program #1			Partnerships	$5,000
Program #2			Downtown Revitalization	$55,000
Program #3			Business Attraction	- 0 -
Program #4			Tourism	$15,000
Program #5			Start-ups	$5,000
Program #6			Gateway	$10,000
Program #7			New Resident Attraction	$20,000
Program #8			Infrastructure	$10,000
Program #9			BRE	$5,000
Program #10			Workforce	- 0 -
Total:	$_____		Total:	$125,000

Voilà! Here's your first-year economic development program budget. Now, take the amounts you've recommended for each program and enter that into the detailed work plans for each strategy. Refine these documents to the point where you are willing to take them to the general public and tell your story. You're off on a great start! Go forth and make things happen for your community.

What Success Looks Like

The town of Field finally had a plan. The groundwork and assessments were done, so the decision about the direction the community would take was fairly easy. Everyone realized that no matter how much they wanted to attract a major industry, that strategy wasn't possible at the present time. Much work would need to be done before they could think about attracting a major employer.

There were positives and negatives to all of the strategies, but the planning group settled on a solution that they felt worked best for all of them. They thought they had developed a sound and implementable plan, and everyone in the community had an opportunity to provide feedback.

The economic development planning group also realized that the plan they decided on was not a finished product. It would change as time progressed, and it would be awhile before they saw the results of their efforts. If they had learned anything in the last six months, it was that economic development took time. Success would be built one job at a time and would grow exponentially today, tomorrow, and into the next generation.

Mayor Rose, who had been in office for less than a year, could already see the community transforming. The planning group had an understanding of the community's unique aspects as well as its shortcomings. Ed, the new economic development director, had expanded his personal skills and knowledge of the profession, and the community had brought together key players to develop a vision and plan for the future.

The Mayor called a special meeting in order to thank all the individuals for their hard work and announce the plan. She had taken the priorities and incorporated them into her budget. Then she began to lay out some possible options.

The town of Field was now ready for economic development.